Hack Your Kids' Education

For Parents Who Are Freaking Out

Hack Your Education Series
Book One

By L. J. Hawke

Dedication

To my editors, alpha and beta readers, and critique partners. Most especially, to all the parents suddenly teaching their kids at home and their amazing kids, thank you. You make my world rock.

Table of Contents

Introduction: Hack Your Kids' Education

By the time this book was near completion, the educational situation in the world had completely changed. One billion children worldwide are now suddenly learning from home. I'm splitting my book into two editions—parents and adult editions. Both are differently informed because of what is happening in the world at the time of this writing.

The world has gone online for business, for work, and now for school. I suspect this may lead to permanent changes. If so, we're going to have to change what we do in terms of educating our youth. During the pandemic, parents and kids must maintain social distance while keeping the ability to maintain relationships with their friends, family members, and neighbors. This time of social isolation can be damaging to young people unless they have an opportunity to work with other people. That can be worked into a curriculum, as well as the opportunity to grow and thrive in academics.

Parents are reeling from all of the changes. I say "parents" to refer to the parent, guardian, extended family member, caregiver, tutor, or even another parent in the same school district educating students. So, when I say "parents," the things in this book can help all of you. Some parents still have to work. They may work in the medical profession, make deliveries, make sure the grocery shelves are stocked and the computers still connect to the Internet. These parents have a harder time making sure their kids get educated. This book is also for anyone helping educate these kids.

Parents are confused. They feel as if they can't do what a teacher does because they don't have the training. Some parents temperamentally find it difficult to work with students on a day-to-day basis. Education is not easy and not always fun at the best of times. This is work. This is a skill that you have to learn to help your students become the best they can be.

Parents who have students with special needs are in even more of a crunch than other parents. Money may already be tight, and now you may have to teach without accommodations that the school can no longer give you. There's a section in this book on this problem.

I'm here to tell you practical things that will get you started. This book has checklists, worksheets, and more to get you started quickly. Use this book like a textbook. Go right to what it is you need to know; it is ok to skip around.

You are not alone. Other parents are going through exactly what you are going through right now. Use this book to kick-start what it is you need to do to educate your kids. You will meet others who are going through the same thing. You can even form groups of local parents working together to educate their students at home. Parents who struggle with students with various learning, brain, and physical differences especially need to band together and exchange tips and tricks on how to teach at home.

The good news is that there's far more out there on the subject than it may seem. People have been homeschooling their students for years. Some have religious, cultural, linguistic, and other situations that make it better for them to homeschool their students. Some have gifted, talented, exceptional, and/or special needs students who work better in a home environment. Some parents live in rural areas, and they don't want their students to travel long distances to school.

Online education allows students to take classes in subjects that their schools may not have. Some people travel all the time because they or their students are actors, sports enthusiasts, artists, or musicians. Some families are in the military, are diplomats, or move around a lot for work. Whatever the reason, there are plenty of people who have done this before you. I'm here to give you as many useful tips and tricks as possible to help you move forward quickly.

I am a university professor. I've been teaching for over a decade. I have taught small children to university students since 2009. I have a master's degree in business administration and a dual master's degree in education and bilingual education, specializing in online education. I am currently teaching my university students remotely at the time this book is being created. I have designed classes and curricula, written a textbook, and taught thousands of hours of classes at this point. I was also a foster mom for four kids. Sadly, I cannot be a foster mom where I am currently located. I do teach kids at an orphanage. I miss my orphan kids terribly; we haven't been able to see each other face-to-face since the crisis began. I have helped my students use numerous resources to hack their own education. You can do this for your kids.

Once you have downloaded the book or obtained the print version, you can go to the website, sign up, and find the checklists and other resources—everything you need in order to get started with your students. The checklists and worksheets in this book will be there for you to download.

There will also be a Facebook group for parents to share what is going on. You have to be able to work together to help your kids learn and to keep your sanity in these confusing times.

Let's get started!

Fast Start: Face to Face Homeschooling

There are a billion students worldwide suddenly sent home due to the coronavirus crisis. Parents are instantly teaching their children even though they have never done this before. These transitions have often been wrenching. Students have suddenly been cut off from their friends and teachers. They may be living in a few rooms without sports, music, or other things that they greatly enjoyed. Both parents and students may be anxious and unsure of the future. Students are very much routine-oriented, and they have been cut off from their old routine.

Then there's the fear and confusion about whether or not this quarter or semester "counts" towards their grades. There is a layer of anxiety on top of everything else about the global pandemic and economic issues. Young students may not be able to understand what exactly is going on, but they can certainly pick up on the anxiety from the people around them. Routine can help diminish free-floating anxiety.

The trick is to create an educational environment that mimics your kids' previous school. This is about schedules, not hallways or lockers. Once you have the schedule, you can then work with your students to make changes if that is better for your particular home environment.

Step One: Get the Textbooks and/or Online Materials

Get all of the resources your students will use, such as textbooks and a list of online materials. This may have been put together in a hurry. If so, don't panic.

Step Two: Find a Copy of Your Student's Schedule

If you have an older student, you may already have access to your student's schedule. This is a great starting point. If not, try to contact the school to get the students' normal schedules.

Your school's website may have your child's schedule. It may cover what subjects students in your child's grade take, and possibly at what times. Try to find the normal lunch and recess times. You may also be able to find information on special things your particular school does, such as a writing prompt at the beginning of every language class and math problems before math class.

You may also be able to find a reading list for your students. A reading list will give you a list of things that your students should have read by the time they're done with their grade.

Graded readers are readers in various subjects such as math, science, biography, history, and more using vocabulary words your students should know or learn. If your school uses graded readers, you should be able to find this out. You can attempt to speak to your students' language teachers or librarians. If your school does use them, you're going to have to find out from the teachers, librarians or your students what their levels are. You can get graded readers online.

You should also be able to determine whether or not your school uses **reverse teaching (flipped classroom)**. **Reverse teaching or a flipped classroom** is when your students' teachers record lessons, and the student then goes to class and does the work where the teacher can see it done. If your school has reverse teaching in most or all of its subjects, then you are off to an excellent start. In this case, you need to find out what the teacher will have the students do in class. For instance, they may have to do problems in the math book or do a short paper on a historical figure. This makes your job as a parent much easier because all you have to do is review the work that your students have to do.

Finding out the schedule will give you a starting point. You don't have to follow it, but it may make students feel more secure, at least in the beginning. You can adjust as you so desire. Keep in mind the *math first principle*. Because that subject has so many concepts and steps that must be taken, your kids have to keep up with that subject, or they fall behind. I suggest doing it first every at-home school day so you won't forget it.

Step Three: Communicate With Your Student's Teacher(s)

You need to contact every teacher your students have. Find out what exactly the teacher does to map out the day. Younger students may have math first, science before lunch, and music after lunch. For older students, knowing their general schedule should be fine.

Does the teacher use reverse/flipped teaching, and, if so, what is assigned in class to do for each video? This type of teaching uses a lot of planning, so the teacher should be able to email you the videos and what the students are supposed to do after they watch them.

Are there worksheets (math, English, science) or writing practice when the student enters the class? If your students do not have any of those special times, you can always put these into your curriculum.

Schedules may change depending on the day of the week. Teachers may have a Monday, Wednesday, Friday schedule, and a Tuesday, Thursday schedule. There may be special things on Fridays, such as field trips, school assemblies, and the like.

Homework

Ask the teachers how they want assignments turned in or recorded. Will you or the teacher review them for errors? Are you simply counting them as completed?

Computer-based work can be uploaded into a special folder and shared with the teacher. If you have a scanner, you can scan your student's offline worksheets and upload them to a folder that you can then share with the teachers. Or, you or your students may take pictures of their work at the end of the school day and upload the pictures into a special online Google Docs folder that is shared with the teachers.

In many school districts, **the parent will be responsible for grading**, not the teacher, unless the teacher explicitly says that they will grade your students' homework.

The idea behind correcting student work is to:
- **Determine whether or not the students understood what it was they were supposed to do based on what they just learned.**
- **Improve for the next assignment.**
- **Find the place where the students can't move forward because they just don't understand the material.** If so, you, as a parent, must help your students understand, use videos that explain the issue, use homework help websites, hire a tutor, or ask the teacher how to instruct your student.

Here are some questions you may want to ask your student's teachers:

For younger students/if the student has one teacher:

- How is the time blocked on a daily basis by subject?
- Are there special subjects like art, music, languages, and programming?
- Are there special pre-teaching things you give or do like writing prompts or math problems?

- ❏ Do you use graded readers? If so, do you know what graded readers my student is reading?
- ❏ Do my students need to turn in book reports? If so, what is the format?
- ❏ Do you have an online folder with all of the handouts or extra materials you plan to use for this quarter or semester? If so, could you share it with myself and other parents in your classes, or upload it to the school's website?
- ❏ Do you do reverse teaching? If so, what is assigned in class to do for each video?
- ❏ How are my students supposed to turn in their work?
    - ❏ Is there a special online folder where you want the work uploaded on the school's website? Or, do you want me to share a folder on Google Docs with you?
    - ❏ Will you review the assignments, or is that my job?

For students with multiple teachers:
- ❏ Are there special pre-teaching items you give or do like writing prompts or math problems?
- ❏ Do you use graded readers? If so, do you know what graded reader my student is reading?
- ❏ Do my students need to turn in book reports? If so, what is the format?
- ❏ Is there a reading list for the books my student should have read by the end of the quarter or semester?
- ❏ Do you have a syllabus for your class that says what you are covering on which day?
- ❏ Do you have an online folder with your syllabus, lesson plans, projects, directions for the projects, and all of the handouts or extra materials you plan to use for this quarter or semester? If so, could you share it with myself and other parents in your classes, or upload it to the school's website?
- ❏ What projects is this class working on, what are the directions, and when are projects due? When and how are the projects supposed to be turned in? How are group projects supposed to be completed?
- ❏ Do you have a list of things my student is supposed to know by the end of the quarter or semester? How to write a report? How to use the scientific method? How to do basic algebra?
- ❏ How are my students supposed to turn in their work?
    - ❏ Is there a special online folder where you want the work uploaded on the school's website? Or, do you want me to share a folder on Google Docs with you?
    - ❏ Will you review the assignments, or is that my job?

Note for school districts, principals, and teachers: Many students throughout the world may not attend school for the rest of the semester, maybe even the entire year. If you don't have the above information ready for parents, prepare it and put it on your school or district website immediately.

Step Four: Determine What Your Student Must Know

If you have textbooks and a syllabus, it should be very clear what your student should know by the end of the quarter or semester. You may be able to contact the manufacturer's website or check online for the teacher's edition of the book if you have no idea how to teach the subject to your students.

If your school is already doing reverse teaching (flipped classroom), then you're in luck. Your students can do their work using reverse teaching (flipped classroom), then do what their teachers require to prove they have learned it. If they don't understand what their teachers are saying, there are dozens of YouTube videos available explaining that same subject in detail. They may simply need it explained differently. If you are a working parent or if the subject confuses you, you can hire a tutor or work with your students' teachers to help your students understand the material.

If there is a reading list, then your students can read whatever the required books are in between their regular classwork, or as part of their language classes. Your students' teachers may be requesting book reports. If so, **find out the format for the book reports**. They are usually the title, the author, the plot, the main characters, the theme, and whether or not and why the student did or didn't enjoy the book. While they are out of regular school, this is a perfect time for students to start reading these lists. [There are several book report examples in the "Checklists, Worksheets, and Projects" section of this book.]

Check library websites in your local area for reading lists by grade level. You can call a librarian or check regional or country requirements with a Google search. **In most countries, there is a rather extensive recommended reading list for high school students to have read by the time they graduate.** If you have a high school or middle school student, you should be able to obtain this list online.

Check the library websites or the apps Libby or Overdrive to find out if your library allows you to check out ebooks and audiobooks online.

The point is to get your students back to school, having learned whatever they needed to learn while the schools are closed. Some parents may decide that an online curriculum helps their students better, and they may switch to an online curriculum then take them out of physical schools permanently. That is up to each family to make that decision.

Step Six: Classwork Help and Tutoring

A simple Google search should come up with numerous videos and websites that will help your students do their schoolwork. They can find videos on YouTube that will walk them through what they just learned. Or, they can go to sites like Math.com, Infostream, and SparkNotes. You don't want a website that will do the work for them. If you want someone who will help students complete their work, try a website like Tutor.com (which is NOT free). There are free homework help tutors out there, especially during the coronavirus crisis. It is important that your students fully understand whatever it is they just read or were asked to do.

Caregivers

If you are a parent that has to work outside the home, your caregiver will have to be teaching, unless you work part-time or on a late shift. If you are legally able to leave your teenager in the house, you may be able to have your self-directed student doing schoolwork while you are at work. I suggest several video check-ins during your day to be sure that your student is fine and doing the work. A homework or tutoring help site can help your student when you are not there. When you return home or the next day before work, check to be sure the work has been done correctly and that the student is on track. With an online school, you can do this with the tools the schools offer.

Tutors

Many teachers or substitute teachers without families of their own who are forced to stay home may be hired as your students' tutors. There may be high school or college students that are able to work as tutors. Remember that older students have their work to do as well.

Remember that your tutor or caregiver will have to wear a mask and possibly gloves while inside the house, or may not be able to come in at all. Explain to your child why this is happening, that the person is following government mandates and is trying to keep everyone safe. Older students will understand an infographic about how coronavirus and other diseases are spread and what they must do to stay safe. This is a fantastic time to teach kids about keeping surfaces clean, as well as frequently washing their hands.

Since you are homeschooling, you can teach your students whenever you want. If you work the second or third shift, you can teach your students when you get home or when you wake up, and use the other people in your life as caregivers, not tutors. You could have your older students sleep when you do, but some may not be able to make their bodies do that.

Try to stick to normal schedules if you can if the students prefer it. Younger kids may only be doing worksheets, songs, and/or educational games for two hours a day, broken up into small blocks. Older kids can probably do all their work in four to six hours, with frequent breaks.

Preparation

Prepare everything for the next day. After all the classwork has been checked, and the kids are in free time or taking a nap, prep for the next day. **The worst time to prepare is at the beginning of the school day.** Doing it the night before saves you time and aggravation.

What textbooks, worksheets, card decks, projects, and supplies do you need? Make sure the kids put all their books and supplies back on their shelves, in their baskets, etc. One good rule is once one activity, game, worksheet, art session, and the like is done, **it must be cleaned up before starting the next one.**

Take prepping to other levels. Do you make a special breakfast with the kids on Wednesdays? Make sure you have all the ingredients the day or even two days before. **Check the calendar for holidays, birthdays, and other special times**, and get the supplies out to make the posters, make the special meal, have the party, or whatever for that day.

You can even prepare meals three times a week for the next few days. For example, cook one chicken or prepare a tofu cake for multiple meals. Wash and cut up vegetables and fruits for snacks and side dishes. Make large side dishes and divide them up for later. If you have a freezer, fill it up with labeled prepped food because some days you just don't want to cook, everyone is exhausted, or whatever. Make pies, cakes, and cookies for a few days with your kids.

Prep meals with your kids. They will learn more about meal planning, and you will teach them some valuable life skills without having to cook all the time. Prep for fun times like pizza nights or pancake breakfasts, or whatever is fun food for your family.

Other Options

School in a Box

School in a Box, otherwise known as a big box or homeschool curriculum, is when textbook companies send books to you, usually separated by grade, possibly by level. They are supposed to cover everything in that grade. If you cannot get textbooks, if your students have zipped past what is in their textbooks, and you do not want to use online or computerized education, this is a good plan for you. Some people live in areas with poor internet, making online learning difficult or even impossible.

With a homeschool curriculum, you can work at your students' paces, teach it however you want, and everything for an entire grade is usually in the box. Many boxes come with teacher's guides.

You will have to go online to find a good school in a box program. Keep in mind your particular situation. You may have a particular preference in religion or want a secular curriculum, be from a certain culture, want your students to learn using multiple languages, or have a part of the curriculum you want to emphasize such as STEAM subjects (science, technology, engineering, art, and math) or environmentalism. School in a box can be passed down from older students to younger ones. Graded readers, science kits, and other projects may be extra.

Investigate using search terms like home school curricula, homeschool curriculum kits, and big box curriculum. Many United States home curriculum producers are Christian-based. If you don't want religion in your textbooks, be sure to find a non-religious company or version. Look for ratings. Join online homeschool parenting groups to find out what they're using and why.

This can be a pricey option. Remember that you will probably be spending $300 or more per child per box.

Note: There is a section in this book about school in a box options.

A hybrid option

There are also curricula that are delivered online that you can print out. This option will use up a lot of paper, but it will be much cheaper than delivering actual books. You can also do this program as a hybrid. Your students can use worksheets when younger, and graduate to the students reviewing the material on the computer. For example, the self-study Robinson Curriculum is $195 for all kids, all grades, K-12. I would highly suggest pairing this hybrid option with library books, ebooks, audiobooks, science kits, languages, art, and music. There are apps for most of the extra things. It is a great way to get started quickly.

Other plans use DVDs or ebooks online to teach directly to the students. One is Teaching Textbooks at www.teachingtextbooks.com. This is a math-only curriculum for grades 2-12. This program is entirely online using ebooks, but you can order the DVDs if you prefer that method. They are kind of lighthearted, and students enjoy being taught directly. This program is $4-$6 per month with discounting for large families.

Putting Together Your Own Curriculum

You can put together your program from online homeschooling resources. However, you run the risk of not covering something your district, state, province, or country requires. You must determine the requirements first. You will also spend a lot of time finding and printing the material. You must be certain your students can pass whatever exams they need to take to graduate from their grade or high school.

I do not recommend this option unless you are an educator because it is time-consuming and somewhat risky that your kids would miss something critical. Some parents use a mishmash of different curricula after finding what works with their kids using trial and error. If you do this method, remember that you are not an expert in everything. You will need to hire tutors or use apps, especially for subjects like music, art, drama, and languages.

Life Skills

Remember that life skills can be taught all along, based on the mental and emotional maturity of students. For instance, five-year-olds can learn to mix the ingredients for bread, but don't have the muscular strength to knead bread and shouldn't be putting food into a hot oven. Cooking is a great life skill to learn!

The good news is that one never knows what will spark a student's interest. There will probably be a lot of trial and error. There is an American commercial that shows a father having his son try and fail various sports, and the father eventually finds out the kid enjoys chess. You can meet the educational requirements from your district, town or city, area, or country while still teaching life skills, covering STEAM (science, technology, engineering, art, and math) courses in a more fun and useful way, and finding what students enjoy and excel at. This is a great time for kids to explore and develop new interests and skills.

Fast Start: Online Learning

If you want to go with the high-quality free English-speaking option, go with the Khan Academy www.khanacademy.org. **Khan Academy also has subtitles in Spanish, French, and Portuguese and offers advanced placement courses and preparation for the SAT college placement exam.** For young kids, ideally, the parental unit or tutor sits next to the students in order to support and encourage them while working on the website. Over time, students will be able to do more and more things on their own, but they will still obviously need an adult in the house in order to feed and support them.

I would suggest starting with the Khan Academy unless you have more money in your budget to spend on your students' education. There are online academies you pay for monthly or yearly, and it can be just like sending your kids to a private school.

Fast Start Scheduling

The Khan Academy has many resources, such as scheduling for kids of different ages and grade levels. Free online schedules are located here: https://keeplearning.khanacademy.org/daily-schedule. There are many other homeschool schedules online, or your online school may have one. Be sure to add in quiet time and free time, and possibly non-electronic time.

Note: There are several schedules included in this book.

School District Learning Academies

It is possible that your school district has already contracted with an online learning academy other than the Khan Academy because some students already learn from home. This may be because there are students who are gifted and talented, with learning or physical differences or speak another language at home, have been bullied, have work (teens), or travel a lot. Whatever the reason, your school district should be able to tell you whether or not they have these contracts. Find out exactly what you have to do to apply, and if the school will pay for it, you have to pay for it, or both.

Online Learning: Research

There are many schools in various countries, some of them doing amazing things with learning using neuroscientific learning methods. Many of them offer excellent academic programs. If you have the funds, you can take advantage of the offerings out there.

If the Khan Academy isn't available in the language you need or if you would rather pay for your children's online education, then there are numerous options available to you. I cannot list them for you, for I don't know what your students' first languages are, the cultures, their religion(s), any learning differences or physical issues, or all the other dynamics that parents will take into account when they choose an online school. To research them, use a search term like "online learning academy K-12" or "online schools K-12," or use the grade your student is in such as "online schools K-6."

Be sure they are fully accredited before doing any further research. See if there are other parents or students that you can speak with online. Find sites that rate these academies, and see if you can find one with a good rating. If you must inform your school, make sure that your school district will accept this particular program as a home-based curriculum. Depending on where you live, you may or may not need to inform your school district at all.

First, look on their websites. Start a notebook sheet or a spreadsheet of their costs, what they offer students, the number of classes that they offer, whether or not they have live teaching or tutoring vs. reverse teaching (flipped classroom), how the students are supposed to do their online work, whether they offer advanced placement and international baccalaureate programs, and the like. **If the school offers live teaching, check your time zones!** You probably don't want your students learning at three in the morning where you are!

Do they offer art, music, drama, and coding classes?

Do they have classes for gifted and talented students, advanced placement classes, and/or an international baccalaureate program?

Be sure that the school placement test and all of the academics are online. You don't want to sign up students for something and find out that they must go somewhere in order to take a certain test or face-to-face program when you can't do that.

You may have to go to your school district and get all of your students' records transferred in an online format before you transfer them to an online academic program that is not the Khan Academy.

Find out if the school offers assistance or tutoring for struggling students, and help for students with learning differences. Is this free or an extra cost? You may have to hire a tutor to help your students.

Find out if you can join anytime, or if you must wait until the next semester. If you start in the middle of a quarter or semester, your students might be behind, struggling to catch up. You may have to enroll your students in an online unaccredited academy or homeschool until the new quarter or semester starts.

Once you have a workable list, let your students in on the decision making. I strongly suggest having your students take virtual tours with you and ask questions if they are old enough. You don't want to start students in schools if it is not the right fit for them.

Once you are certain you've made the right decision, get your students enrolled as soon as possible, or get them in the Khan Academy immediately and keep them there until the next school semester or quarter starts.

Supervision

Remember that your students must have supervision. Check with your area, district, city, region, or country to determine how old a student may be to be alone in the house while you are working. If you must work outside of the house, then you are going to have to make certain that someone is there with your students. If you do so, during the pandemic, you may have to hire someone that wears a mask and gloves inside your home. Explain about government regulations so your students are not frightened by this.

The point of a tutor is to sit next to your students and offer encouragement for young children. For older children, the point would be to be in the same room and to offer academic help and encouragement throughout the day. Of course, the tutor should be certain your students are getting food and fluids and plenty of breaks. All students, including older ones, do need breaks and playtime in order to reset the brain so that they can refocus later.

Extra Online Learning

Music, Art, Film, and Drama

This is a fantastic time for students to learn to play a musical instrument. If you are in an apartment that is not soundproofed, you are probably going to have to make sure your students are learning from electronic instruments that can plug into earphones, such as electronic drums or keyboards. If soundproofing isn't a problem, students can choose other instruments. They can learn from apps, YouTube, or instructors that are outside the home that they see on a video monitor. Students who want to pursue art such as painting and calligraphy can also take these classes on YouTube and from online tutors.

Encourage all students to learn how to read music and how to do simple drawings such as icons. Many students use icons to help them take notes. This is a fast way to study later on; the icons are little "codes" the brain uses to quickly determine what is important.

Encourage music, art, and film and/or theater appreciation classes for older students. Those courses have been invaluable to help people appreciate the arts. This is a fantastic time to read plays and see them performed online, or to develop an appreciation of old movies.

Languages

It is extremely important for you to be certain your students take another language so they can survive in a global economy. There are thousands of them to choose from. The ones that are spoken by the most people are English, Mandarin Chinese, Arabic, Spanish, Hindustani, Malay, Russian, Bengali, Portuguese, and French.

Students choose languages to learn for a variety of reasons such as their cultural history, the region where they are living, to get a job in the future, or because they feel a language and culture is interesting. Work with your students to choose one and start immediately. Dyslexic students often choose Chinese as an ideographic language, or Arabic because it is read from right to left instead of from left to right. **Students can learn nearly any language online for free** through their online academy, YouTube, numerous free or low-cost apps, or free courses through Udemy. This is the perfect time to get them started with language learning!

Linguistic Volunteering

Translation is a great way for students to learn other languages. If you would like to do free translation work, I would contact the Khan Academy about translating their coursework into the languages of your country. One of my students began working for Google once I suggested he start translating videos into his native language.

If you are a philanthropist and you have serious funds, I would approach the Khan Academy about subtitles for many more languages. If you are a developer with a speech translation program translating speech from English into languages such as Chinese, Arabic, or Russian, I would approach the Khan Academy about translating the many hours of speech they have in their lessons. It would be a great test of your translation software, and great advertising for you if you're able to do it for them for free!

It may seem like I tout Khan Academy. It is a great free resource that I encourage you to take advantage of, including to enrich another curriculum.

Fast Start: Face to Face Teaching

At this point, you should have the textbooks that your students use. If you're lucky, you also have a schedule, possibly a syllabus, and possibly worksheets and projects.

What to Do With Younger Kids

Younger kids like bright colors, shapes, and movement. They like songs and music. They like to have fun. The ideas to make school as fun as you can make it.

In the beginning, try to follow the schedule that the teacher uses. If you haven't been able to contact the teacher, don't panic. Ask your kids what they do at school. If you can, ask the other parents. If your student does not have a textbook, try to contact the teacher to get the worksheets that the teacher was going to use. You may be able to contact the school or the district to find out what students are supposed to learn in your students' grades. If you don't have any of that, don't panic.

No Textbook (Online or Offline) With Worksheets

Try to make your child's schedule the way it was at school, with math time, reading, science, and lots of play. If your students are preschoolers or kindergarteners, teachers may teach by talking or demonstrations, possibly on a whiteboard, then test their students with in-class assignments (worksheets). Preschool teachers are teaching letters, numbers, words, movement, music, art, and comparatives like big and small. They read stories to students, preferably with special voices for each character.

There is a huge growth in the brain between ages four and five for students who are able to do far more than they used to be able to do. They are able to learn how to read and write, and read and write their first sentences. They are able to think through things like addition and subtraction in terms of having two apples and taking away one apple.

There are hundreds of worksheets available online for preschool and kindergarten teachers, and plenty of academic videos on YouTube and other websites to help you teach your child. Remember to back up learning videos like those on numbers and letters with a worksheet so that you know they understand what it is they just saw. Television shows like *Reading Rainbow* and *Between the Lions* read books to kids. There is a lot of material online if you look for it.

If you need to print out worksheets and if you have a printer at home, buy a lot of paper and far more printer ink than you think you're going to need. If you don't have a printer, find the worksheets for free online at websites like Scholastic and home education websites. Download them onto your computer, then move the worksheets you like into a folder.

If you don't have a printer at home, check with your local printing service and find out if they will print (and possibly deliver) a stack of worksheets to you if you share the folder with them. Be sure to tell them whether or not you want black and white or color. Color worksheets are going to cost more money.

You will probably vastly underestimate how many worksheets you need. If you're teaching several different subjects, you may teach five of them a day. You may also need **manipulatives,** physical objects to teach math, science, and other things. You can buy kits, like word blocks your kids use to make sentences. Or you can make your own!

Scan or take a picture of all of your students' work and put it in a folder so you have a record for the teacher or school district of what has been done. This is a good idea, even for very young students.

There is a much cheaper alternative to printing out worksheets. The Khan Academy teaches students from 4-18 years old in English **for free**.

Older Kids

Older kids should have textbooks or online books, reading lists, project lists, and possibly syllabi. Try to cover two to four pages per day per subject. You may find they like to study at places other than the kitchen table, such as in their room or propped up on pillows on the floor. These students probably need a comfortable chair where they can curl up and a clipboard or lap desk so they can work anywhere.

If your kids have cell phones, they can use them for academic purposes during the school day, such as looking up words or watching a YouTube video on how to do a math problem. Make sure they can make calls to their friends when not doing schoolwork through Zoom, Skype, or other free communication programs.

There are some wonderful educational YouTube series like *Crash Course* and *SciShow*. Please check out this content. *Crash Course* teaches so many subjects, like history, anatomy and physiology, biology, economics, and much more. There are guides on Teachers Pay Teachers for these shows. You do not have to buy the guides, but they do provide a framework for learning.

Computer Time

If you don't have a separate work and student computer, the Khan Academy may not work for you. If you have the funds, you may be able to order a cheap tablet computer for $100 or less and have your student do the work on a tablet. Check online shopping in your area, discount stores, and electronic boards like Craigslist to find used computers.

Your student doesn't need a top-of-the-line gaming computer to do academic work and projects such as podcasts and videos. **Your smartphone is a computer!** If your students have smartphones, they may be able to do a great deal of their academic work on them. You can buy keyboards that work with the cell phones that will allow them to type into Google Docs if you can't get a computer right now.

Offices upgrade their computers all the time; check with businesses that want to sell their old ones. Computer repair shops may have refurbished computers. You can also take out an ad asking for someone to donate an old computer to your students. You may be able to talk with community organizations or even computer manufacturers to get you a free or discounted computer if you need a computer for your students and you don't have the budget because of the crisis. Of course, you're going to have to disinfect anything you buy. There are special wipes and sprays for computers that will help you do that.

Your students can simply do everything offline with paper and pencil. Young children especially may prefer it that way!

Textbook With No Syllabus

If you have a textbook with no syllabus, just divide up the book into two to four pages a day. You can cut up the time into half pages if you want to. If students run into things they don't understand, they can stop and watch a video on that particular subject on YouTube. There are also numerous videos and podcasts available for students to learn about certain subjects, many of them created by and for other students. **You must make sure your students are actually looking at academic things, not watching cute cat videos or playing video games.**

If your textbook has a companion workbook, then you don't need extra worksheets. You can always look online for a companion workbook if your school doesn't provide one. If there is a teacher's book for the textbook, you can have it sent to you so that you can be a better teacher. It may be available online. Check and see if the textbook manufacturer has videos or other materials available to students who use that particular textbook.

Let your students go at their paces. Just be sure they do math first and do at least one to two complete pages. Math is a cumulative subject, and it has to be done every day. I recommend you do it first because it is like building a wall. If you skip anything, it is like missing a brick or stone in the wall or the mortar that holds it together. If your kids really do better with math later in the day, then that is fine, but don't skip it entirely.

You may be surprised to find that kids are zipping through the textbooks. The district's school day is full of distractions and things like fire drills and assemblies. Your students will be free from these distractions but may have different ones, such as dealing with a loud little brother or sister.

There are numerous projects you can assign your kids to be sure they understand the material. If the students' teachers haven't assigned homework, papers, or anything of the kind, you can do that yourself. **The point is for the students to be able to prove they have learned the material**, preferably in an interesting way, by writing a report, reading a book and doing a book report, creating a game, video, or podcast. Students generally have to write a script for a podcast. Kids can create podcasts or videos about nearly any academic subject and still be using language arts skills.

Cross assignments that combine multiple subjects can be beneficial. For instance, you may combine language arts and history by having your students come up with a podcast or video about a certain time in the past in your region or country. Students may be able to do these projects in groups with their friends via phone or video chat. This is a great way to have your students stay in touch with their friends, as well as learn how to use technology. It is relatively easy to merge math, science, and technology into projects. Lists of projects can be found on many homeschooling websites. Communicate with your students' teachers or other parents to devise these assignments.

Textbook With A Syllabus

If the teachers have both the textbooks and the syllabi, you and your students know exactly what they're supposed to be learning on any particular day. If there are assignment project sheets, you also know what your students are supposed to be doing to prove that they have covered the subject matter. As long as they can prove that they understand what it is they've just covered, let your kids go as fast as they want. If they go slow, on the other hand, it means you probably have to give extra help or get a tutor to help. Students have different brains, different study patterns, different ways of learning. Many kids find the textbooks incredibly boring and are able to understand better with YouTube videos and educational podcasts and games about that particular subject.

Decoding The Syllabus

A **syllabus** is a merging of assignments and dates (or weeks of a semester or quarter). For instance, this is a small part of one of my syllabi:

Week 1: Pages 4-6, classwork page 8
Week 2: Pages 9-11, classwork page 13, overview Final Presentation, choose topic

Teachers use syllabi to plan their semester. They may design their own or may receive them from the school, other teachers, or the school district. They are generally not shared with students until late high school. If you have one or your students' teachers are willing to share them with you, then you are lucky. They come in a wide variety of formats. Some have an actual calendar. Most are just lists of dates. I include the URLs of websites and videos that I use in class. My students use them to peek ahead and be sure they are on track for all projects.

With syllabi, you know what your students must cover by the end of the quarter or semester. You don't have to follow it exactly by date.

Reverse Teaching/Flipped Classrooms

If your students are already doing **reverse teaching (flipped classrooms)** where the students see a video then do an assignment, then you are very lucky because most of the work has been done for you. You need to know what your students need to do in order to prove to the teacher they understand the subject matter. Your students' teachers should be able to tell you what that is for each video, such as being able to do the problems on page six of their textbook. Students can use YouTube videos if they don't understand their teachers' videos. You may need to help your student or get an online tutor if your student is going very slowly or is extremely frustrated.

Perfectionism

At this point, just making sure that your students understand what it is they need to know in order to pass their grade is the most important thing during the coronavirus outbreak. You don't want to be a so-called "tiger parent" and make sure your students are doing every assignment perfectly. Remember, your students are under stress too. If you're that concerned about your kids falling behind, you'll probably want to enroll your students in an online school or consider school in a box.

Scheduling

In order to make students feel safe and doing something that they're used to doing, try to follow the schedule that the school has. You don't have to stick with the school schedule if it doesn't work for your kids. If your students prefer math, then science, followed by music and dancing, then do that. You may also end up having students from several grade levels in the house, and that may cause conflicts. If it is easier to have everyone doing the same subjects at the same time, then do that.

Fast Start: Scheduling

The Khan Academy has many resources, such as scheduling for kids of different ages and grade levels. Free online schedules are located here: https://keeplearning.khanacademy.org/daily-schedule. There are also dozens of scheduling examples online.

Note: This book includes several schedules you can use.

Attention Span

Young students have an attention span of between 5 to 15 minutes. Older ones may be able to hold out for a little bit longer. **Generally speaking, the Pomodoro method of 10-25-minute learning blocks is the best method to teach in order to retain information.** There are plenty of free Pomodoro timers that go off after the time that you set them, such as for 10 or 15 minutes.

Prepare a batch of all the different things that your students need to use to learn, such as textbooks, worksheets, and the like. Have them work for whatever time you have set, and then give them 5 minutes off. If they finish before the bell rings, give them something else to work on. Then they can switch or stay on the same subject for another round.

I would suggest students get 15 minutes playtime at the end of each hour, half an hour off at the end of every two hours, and a full hour off after every four hours. Remember to keep them in drinks and snacks throughout this time, with snacks every two hours, and usually a meal every four hours.

Academic Child Development Websites

Academic child development websites can explain what it is a child is supposed to do academically at what age. Don't worry about doing a deep dive into all of the research. You should be able to know most of this by knowing your students' grade levels. The reason why students are divided by age is to have students with the same general development together.

You don't want to push your students to work beyond their level. That actually doesn't mean that much, because there's always going to be 10% of the students that are behind, 10% that are way ahead, and the middle that just do what is in front of them. Then there's 10% that have some sort of brain, learning, or linguistic difference or medical issue affecting learning that has to be addressed. (Do you see why teachers have such difficult jobs? In many schools, 30% of our students have different needs from the other 70%!)

School Day vs. Home Time

You will probably discover that the school day of six to eight hours is ridiculous compared to learning at home. Remember, in a regular school, kids have to go from class to class. There are numerous distractions throughout the day. In the United States, there is a whole lot of academic testing that takes up a great deal of time. Unless you're lucky enough to be in an excellent school district or a private school, your students' teachers have to deal with anywhere between 20 and 70 other students, depending on where you live in the world. Remember the 10% blocks of students who are way ahead and students who are behind? Also, students with special needs may need constant redirection or supervision. All of that takes class time away from your students. **Working one-on-one means your students can progress much faster than they would in a regular school.**

Student Differences

The good news about working at home is that you have control over your students' environment. If you already know your students have academic or medical issues, then you probably know what you need to do. If your students have sensory processing disorders, you're going to have to put them in an environment that is quiet and maybe even somewhat dark. If you have students with ADHD, you know you're going to have to set a timer that goes off every ten minutes and have lots of play/movement periods interspersed throughout the day.

If you have no idea what to do, your students' special education teachers can help you. *Immediately go online and find other parents whose students have the same issues.* They are going through what you're going through. Type in the name of the issue or disorder and "other parents dealing with" to find websites, information, and social media such as Facebook groups. You will be stunned by the tips and tricks you can learn from other parents. They may even have free online Skype or Zoom calls to help each other. They may also use online communication apps that have "rooms" such as Slack and Discord. If they use communication apps you're not used to using, watch free videos on YouTube that explain how to use them before downloading them to your phones or computers.

Let me use myself as an example. I have attention deficit disorder or ADD. It means I can only concentrate on something for about 25 minutes at the most as an adult before my brain skips. Other times, I have what I call hyper-focus. I'm able to concentrate on something for hours if it is something I'm highly interested in or passionate about. I call that "going down the rabbit hole." Students on the autism spectrum usually do the same thing. I know this is a problem with the level of dopamine in my brain. Dopamine is the brain chemical related to focus. So, I can do dopamine-enhancing tasks such as short five to fifteen-minute things that are easy to complete. Or, I can play a video game or read a book for up to fifteen minutes before I tackle a difficult task. **Once you know how your students' brains work academically and with dopamine levels, you can figure out how to best teach your students.**

Fast Start: Organization

Advance Preparation

If you want to prepare learning for the week, print out and put together the worksheets for a week in a folder organized by day or subject. You can teach five days a week, and take days off when you want. You may choose to have Wednesday and Saturday or Sunday off rather than weekends. Some parents plan two or even four weeks in advance. Buy a few clipboards so kids can do them curled up in a bed, lying on the floor, in a hammock, or whatever.

Do NOT date the folders. Homeschooled students tend to work ahead, or may need to slow down to understand a difficult concept. You can write down days of the week on the folders. Unfinished papers can be moved into the next day's folder without difficulty.

Next, take the worksheets for each subject out and put them in a binder for each day. Slide them into clear or colored plastic paper holders organized by subject. Or, put them on a clipboard, or leave the folder on the students' desks. The students then learn either via textbooks or online at whatever time of day they do that subject. Some students will just keep doing checklists or going through their folders or clipboards until they are finished for the day. Do whatever works for you and your students.

Know Your Students

Knowing your students is the key to their education. Work on the more difficult subjects for five to fifteen minutes at a time, switch them, and discover what subjects send your students down the rabbit hole of deep interest. Once you find the "rabbit hole" subjects, schedule those at the end of the day and finish all the other academic subjects before you get there. Then, they can dive as deep as they want.

Internet

If you are unable to pay an internet bill, remember that you may be able to combine your internet and your phone service. You may also be able to use your cell phone as a VPN (virtual private network) in order for your laptop or tablet to be able to receive the Internet. There are videos online that will tell you how to do this. It is possible that your internet service company may be able to allow you to not pay a bill for a few months during the crisis if you can prove you have students at home. If you have to, copy or take a photo of whatever it is your students are doing and upload it to a folder on your cell phone. You can use that to prove to the school district that you are teaching your students. Community organizations or even corporations may be able to help you with paying for home internet access.

There is wifi everywhere. Don't go against the government instructions and leave your house. If you're able to do so, put a mask on, keep social distance, and bring your laptop, tablet, or cell phone with you. You may be able to go to or outside a coffee shop and work off the internet there. You may be surprised at the number of places that have internet access. Work offline and upload your students' work once a week. If the local coffee shop is closed, either take pictures of the students' work and upload it later, or keep it by week or month by subject in folders or packets to bring back to school when it opens again.

For those of us who are lucky enough to have a steady income during this crisis with funds left over, see if there is a way that low-income families can be helped to have internet and computer services during lockdowns in your area.

Homeschooling Websites

There are numerous homeschooling and homeschooling association websites available all over the world in multiple languages. I would check out Scholastic (they sell books, look under Teaching Tools) and the Home Schooling Association (there are many USA state-run associations; I like California's association). There are many more based on religions, cultures, and languages. You will need to do your research if you are looking for a specific kind of homeschool association.

Informational and Tutoring Websites

Sites like Sparknotes and Math.com can help your students study and get help for specific questions. Tutor.com has actual tutors to teach your students online in 80 subjects. They offer a free tutoring session; you must pay for the rest. You can keep costs down by waiting until your student has a specific problem and an exploration of YouTube videos and searches on sites like SparkNotes and FactMonster.com have not helped.

Fast Start: Supplies and Environment

How do I make the environment great for my students?

This depends on where your students like to study. Some students prefer to study in their bedrooms, either at their desks or on their beds. Some prefer to use the family kitchen table. Some prefer to work in the family room or home office. Some like to rotate; let them do it. **Make sure there is at least one comfortable or squishy chair where kids can curl up and read**. A great project is to make posters for the walls. Another is to make your lap desk from cardboard and a pillow. They may want to lie on pillows on the floor and write on clipboards or lap desks.

Tailor the environment to your students. Kids with sensory disorders like learning in very monochromatic, dim environments. ADD/ADHD kids will want to circulate around. Know your students, ask questions, and let them find their "new normal."

Discount or dollar stores: Buy supplies there if you have a discount store near you!

What supplies do I need?

This depends on the age of your students. I would strongly suggest this supply list.

Basic supplies:
- Tissues
- Hand soap
- Sanitizer gel
- Pens
- Pencils
- Pencil sharpener OR lead for refillable pencils
- Erasers
- Pencil pouch
- Notebooks
- Glue stick
- Craft sticks
- Clothespins or binder clips
- Sticky notes
- Dry erase pens in a variety of colors and erasers
- Clear plastic page protectors
- Craft paper

- ❏ Dabbers for bingo (they stamp a circle of color)
- ❏ Stickers, stars, or tokens such as superhero magnets for chore and behavior charts
- ❏ Plastic table covers (helpful for crafts)
- ❏ Wooden stamps and a stamp pad (this is an extra, but really useful)
- ❏ For elementary students (starting around age 6-7)–Calendar, calendar app, or BUJO (bullet journal you can build and adapt; there are dozens of videos on YouTube on how to make your own or buy one)
- ❏ Calculator, unless your student has a smartphone or computer
- ❏ Lap desk. You can order one online, or make one out of a perfectly-sized pillow, and glue a flat board or doubled-over cardboard wrapped with contact paper to the top of a pillowcase.
- ❏ Clipboards for each kid. You can make one from a piece of hard plastic or thin sanded wood and clothespins.

Art supplies for young students:
- ❏ Colored pencils
- ❏ Crayons
- ❏ Finger paints
- ❏ Butcher, whiteboard, or chalk paper–you can buy a roll of whiteboard paper you can erase over and over from Amazon.com. You can order chalkboard paper, but chalk is not good for the lungs. Buy a whiteboard, or for a fun project, tear apart a cardboard box and cover the segments with whiteboard or chalk contact paper.
- ❏ Whiteboard pens
- ❏ Colored pens
- ❏ Stickers. (Lots and lots of stickers.)
- ❏ Coloring books
- ❏ Play dough or reusable colored clay
- ❏ Glitter glue, NOT glitter. Glitter gets everywhere and is very hard to clean up.
- ❏ **Note:** There are slime and playdough recipes online. I have included a checklist for the items that usually go into some of the most common recipes in this book.

Basic Supplies: Older Students
- ❏ Colored pencils
- ❏ Colored pens
- ❏ Erasers
- ❏ Pencil sharpener OR lead for refillable pencils
- ❏ Pencil case or box
- ❏ Glue stick

- ❏ Notecards
- ❏ Graph paper
- ❏ Hole punch
- ❏ Protractor
- ❏ Sticky notes
- ❏ Binder
- ❏ Correction tape
- ❏ Folders
- ❏ Paper clips
- ❏ Highlighters in multiple colors
- ❏ Calendar, calendar app, or BUJO (bullet journal you can build and adapt)
- ❏ Scientific calculator–unless your student has a smartphone or computer
- ❏ Scrap paper for notes or checklists, checklist paper if you can find it, and/or the new electronic pens and clipboards that allow you to take notes or draw and upload the work to your computer or cellphone (saves on paper AND keeps an electronic record)

Fun Supplies

- ❏ Drawing paper or adult coloring books (use computer or tracing paper so the books can be used multiple times)
- ❏ Stencils
- ❏ Journal or bullet journal–create your own as a great project (use YouTube videos)
- ❏ Drawing/Painting supplies–I suggest colored pencils for less mess. Watercolors are fine. Don't buy an expensive painting kit unless your students want to learn painting.
- ❏ Slime/dough ingredients–look up recipes on the Internet
- ❏ Magnetic tape and magnets. If you can find them, superhero or other magnets kids love are great for chore charts and behavior tokens. I use small colorful circular magnets I bought at a discount home supply store.

Organizational Supplies (desired, not must have):

- ❏ Cubed bookcase so you can insert baskets (You can create one out of plastic cubes.)
- ❏ Outbox, folders, or plastic sheet covers for completed sheets
- ❏ Hanging file, crate with folders, or other places to file completed exams, projects, or sheets. File by child. Keep to prove what your kids have done. If you are doing an online curriculum, this is probably unnecessary.
- ❏ Baskets or bins

- ❏ Cups for pens
- ❏ Small baskets or plastic containers for smaller supplies
- ❏ Clipboards
- ❏ Folders
- ❏ Binder clips
- ❏ Plastic sheet covers, some clear, some in various colors

Tip: Have one art supply box and one school box per child so they don't whine about whose supplies are whose.

Electronics
- ❏ Computer–laptop, tablet, netbook or smartphone
- ❏ Scanner or take pictures of offline schoolwork via your phone
- ❏ Calculator unless you're using a smartphone or computer
- ❏ Earphones
- ❏ Wifi router
- ❏ Internet service
- ❏ **Keyboard (if your laptop has sticky or missing keys, or to use on your lap)**–I use the slim, ergonomic wireless Moko Bluetooth keyboard I got for about $26 on Amazon. I use an ergonomic keyboard because it is less strain on my fingers, and I can use it on my lap. Dvorak or other keyboards are even more ergonomic, but there is a learning curve to learn how to type on them. Kids love gaming keyboards that light up.
- ❏ **Apps**–there are apps for taking notes, like EverNote and Bear, Pomodoro timers to keep track of time, apps that let you record audio and video, and many more. Be careful to select free ones if budget is an issue, and make sure the apps are used tools. Delete unused ones.
- ❏ **Google Extensions**–there are great free extensions like ad blockers, virtual private networks (VPNs), and parental controls. The free version of Nimbus lets you take screenshots, and for about $15 a year will let you take videos and download them as MP4s.
- ❏ **Check rating sites for all apps and extensions** to find the ones that are simple and easy to use.
- ❏ **Notion** is a powerful productivity app. It is not free, and you can easily go down a rabbit hole of finding out all its uses. But, it is a great all-in-one notetaker, database manager, calendar app (including kanban), checklist and to-do list manager, and more. If you need one app to rule them all, you can check this one out.

Exercise:

- ❑ Yoga mats (go thick for young students)
- ❑ Exercise bands
- ❑ Hula hoops
- ❑ Very light weights (you can use water bottles or cans) for teens
- ❑ A phone or laptop to use videos. This is a GREAT time to learn yoga, Zumba, or tai chi.

Music:

Small children–you can buy a little kit for toddlers with a triangle, tiny drum, tambourine, and maracas. It is really fun to dance around and play these simple instruments.

Older kids–the cheapest ones are the recorder, harmonica, and ocarina (a little flute).

Expensive ones–keyboard or electronic drum set, with earphones

Still relatively cheap–guitar, ukulele, flute

Where to get: Online or locally

You may be able to buy used instruments from pawn shops. You may be able to rent them. Remember to disinfect them!

Instrument teaching apps: There are plenty of them online for the keyboard/piano, guitar, drums, and more.

Board Games

- Board games teach numbers, letters, shapes, and strategic thinking.
- Toddlers can learn rules and will learn games for older kids faster than you think. If you want to play more adult games, reserve those for when toddlers go to sleep.
- Take your time building a game library. Start with cheaper card games like Uno and save the expensive ones for when you can afford them. If you have the funds, buy them all!
- WATCH OUT FOR CHOKING HAZARDS. Toddlers will eat small pieces like marbles or put them in their noses or ears. Watch your little ones at all times!

Young kids: Candyland, Chutes and Ladders, Sleeping Queens, Go Fish, Go Fish Alphabet, Gobblet Gobblers, Zingo, Ruckus, Hoot Owl Hoot, Richard Scarry's Busytown, Robot Turtles, Feed the Kitty, Stack Up!

Elementary: Uno, Junior Skip-Bo, Skip-Bo, Parcheesi, Checkers, Sleeping Queens, Outfoxed, Sushi Go, Zingo, Tsuro, Rat-A-Tat-Cat, Spot It! Jr. Animals, Spot It!, Go Fish, Ticket to Ride First Journey, Ticket to Ride, My First Carcassonne, Qwirkle, dominoes,

Labyrinth, Dixit, Otrio, Yahtzee, Jenga, Blokus, Taco Cat Goat Cheese Pizza, Tenzi, Q-bitz

Older Elementary/Middle School: Clue, Monopoly, Chess, backgammon, Rummikub. Carcassonne, Sequence, Catan Junior

High School and Up: Catan, Risk, Legendary, Takenoko, Steampunk Rally, Quantum, Terraforming Mars, Quadropolis, Five Tribes, Codenames, Apples to Apples, Mombasa, Orleans, Runewars, StarCraft, Falling Sky

This is just a starter list. There are many games out there. Check online gaming (and parenting) boards, videos, and sites to find out which ones gamers and parents rate highly. New ones are being invented all the time!

Project: Why don't you have your students invent their own games? Kids can make action, dance, dice, card, or board games themselves.

To make a card game, get some heavy construction paper and trace out card outlines. Kids can make flashcards, icon cards, any kind of card they want. Laminate them or use clear glue and plastic sleeves to cover them. Let them make their own rules, then have them write them down. Or, have them teach you how to play and write the rules down yourself.

To create a board game, you need a square or rectangle of cardboard covered with contact or construction paper. Your board can be a magical kingdom, an island, a spaceship, whatever you want! You can draw on your board, or if you have a printer, print out an image or images you copy or design.

You can make game pieces out of plastic toys, paper tubes, egg cartons, or plastic bottles, cut out or fold origami ones, make them from play dough, or order online from someplace like Etsy. You can also buy something called Inkjet Shrink Film; use this if you have both an inkjet printer and an oven at home. To use, find an image you want to use, double its size, print it out on the inkjet printer, and bake according to the directions.

Look up "DIY game pieces" or "how to make custom game pieces" online or on YouTube to make them out of dough or other materials. That's how lots of real-life games got started!

Note: This section on games is found elsewhere in the book as well.

Fast Start: Small Group Learning

Small Group Learning for Kids

Students need to be socialized. Some kids work better alone, and some better in groups. Students can learn by teaching others. There are many ways to go about dealing with this.

Homeschool Small Learning Groups

Get involved in a small learning group. You can try to find other homeschoolers in your area. First, contact your students' former classmates. Students can tutor each other, give each other homework help (without doing homework for each other), and do projects together. Older students can help other younger ones.

Neuroatypical students can greatly benefit from finding another student in your area with the same difference or cluster of differences. Neuroatypical students tend to do better with other neuroatypical people. Just having someone who understands, who won't force you into a conversation you don't want or ask questions you don't know how to answer, can be the best thing in the world.

Virtual Groups

There are virtual choirs and bands, board gaming and crafts groups, movie, music, or book clubs, bullet journal or scrapbooking clubs, and more. These groups may meet on Zoom or social media, and may even create videos or podcasts for others. Look for these groups online. Find activities your kids enjoy and find a group, or make your own!

Parent Groups

Parents can work together to homeschool their children. Start with the other parents in your kids' classes, or with your friends with kids. Parents do not need to have students in the same classes, using the same study materials, or even be the same ages. Sometimes parents work part-time jobs, and only need a study group for their kids in the morning or afternoon. They can work with other parents with tips, tricks, information about the school or class, or just help each other get through the situation.

Meetings

Talk on the phone with other parents at least twice a week. Students may need to talk to their friends more often. This is especially helpful when the kids are starting to go stir crazy, locked in the house for too long.

Field Trips

Virtual Field Trips

Field trips have to be virtual for now. There are many museums, zoos, aquariums, historical sites, farms, planetariums, national parks, and governmental websites that have them online. Type "virtual field trips" into Google and Youtube to start. Students can do reports on their visits to these sites for science, history, and language classes.

Once the social distancing rules ease, you can work with other homeschooling parents to go on activities together, like touring a botanical garden, working with an animal rescue society, or going to a local museum. Volunteering is also an excellent way for your kids to meet others. You could do all of these things yourselves, but working with other parents gives homeschooling parents the ability to make friends of their own, not just the students. Part of the point of homeschooling is being able to take those opportunities. You can go hiking, camping, swimming, horseback riding, and all sorts of other activities on your schedule and based on your interests.

Warning: Once social distancing rules ease, bring your homeschooling letter or whatever it is you need if you are out and about during local school hours. Also, be sure you have the right number and kind of car seats in the car if you're transporting young children with your vehicle.

After School Activities

Once social distancing rules ease, there are many after-school activities that allow students of all ages to participate in your community. Check out the local community center, or after-school activities at the local school. This can be anything from swimming to chess, basketball to martial arts. There are also Boys & Girls Clubs, Boy and Girl Scouts, Camp Fire groups, and cultural, ethnic, and religious organizations that have activities for kids as well. These classes, activities, and groups are a great way for students to get to know each other and to do activities that they enjoy together.

If you are part of a homeschool small learning group, perhaps a group of kids can attend these activities together. Your student can also take a pottery class, learn to ride a horse, learn a martial art, or go to the local climbing wall. Many students learn how to play musical instruments on YouTube, and can get together in small bands, or even join a marching or other band.

These activities can be very enriching for students, and it helps get them out of the house. Once social distancing rules ease, this will be very important to them. Students get to learn how to deal with other students in interactions surrounding an activity, hobby, or sport, which makes it far easier for them to have conversations. This can be especially helpful with neuroatypical children, who have to learn to deal with people with different kinds of brains. **Be sure the instructor knows of any issues beforehand, and stay close by or even take your own class in the same place if your student is neuroatypical or has issues with other children.**

Camps and Virtual Camps

There are online camps for students in STEAM, coding, and more. There is a mix of free and for-cost programs available online. Kanopy is a free library-based program. MarcoPolo World School is an app, free to try, then you pay a fee. This allows students to view a video, then play an educational game on that topic. DIY and Make Online are activity-based sites with projects. You have to pay for the materials, but this is a great way to keep kids occupied. PBS Kids for Parents also has activities. Google has a Made With Code site to get teen girls to code and compose music. Google Arts and Culture has free activities and information. CreativeLive has educational video courses aimed at tweens and teens. Type "virtual camps" into Google.

Once social distancing rules ease, students can attend real-life camps, like robotics or swimming camps. There are camps for kids with specific physical, mental, and emotional differences, as well as for those who are neuroatypical. These camps are generally offered in the summers, but in warmer climates, they may be offered over winter breaks. In colder climates, there are camps for winter sports. There are also camps offered by ethnic and religious organizations. The idea is to help your students learn new skills by doing fun activities and make new friends. Check for scholarships and special programs for low-income families for kids to attend these camps. If you have the funds, consider providing a scholarship.

Camps often give parents a much-needed break while giving kids a chance to let loose outside the house. But, very shy kids or ones that have never been away from home before should not be forced to attend a camp when they don't want to go. It might be better for them to attend a day camp where they do not have to sleep outside the home. Neuroatypical students should not be forced to attend camp with students with other types of brains if it will make their problems worse, like triggering anxiety or obsessive-compulsive disorder. **It is better for neuroatypical students to attend camps with other neuroatypical students, or to attend day camps only.**

Warning: Camps can be expensive. Look for scholarships or other special programs. Children with severe allergies, such as to bee stings, should only attend indoor camps. It is very difficult to regulate a child's diet at camp or have a child take medications at specific times throughout the day unless the camp specifically caters to these children. Also, just because you have happy memories of attending a camp in your childhood, your child may not feel the same way. Everyone's brain is different. Be sure the camp dovetails with your student's interests, not your own. Your job is to raise a happy, healthy child.

Fast Start: The Differently-abled

The fact that the differently-abled are not able to go to school puts parents in an extremely difficult, even untenable position. These parents have even more of a need to bring home money for their kids. Parents may have to work in jobs such as nurse, delivery driver, or power plant worker. These parents must take extreme caution at work so they do not bring home any contagious diseases because people with differing abilities may have immune problems.

The different needs of students are on a spectrum, running the gamut from the student with the extremely mild intellectual or brain differences to students in wheelchairs, with seizure disorders, or any other special needs. In addition, schools often offer free lunches and even occupational or speech therapy for students that they will no longer have at home.

Here are some tips:

Contact your students' teachers. Make sure you understand exactly what they do during the day at what time. However, your student may hate the school's schedule and be frustrated with no ability to change it. Now is your opportunity to move things around.

Use alarms and transition times. There are Pomodoro apps you can set to go off, usually in 10-25-minute blocks with five to ten minutes off in between, but you can make the blocks shorter. Use music or headphones or a certain mouse pad you switch when you move from one subject to another. Use alarms to remind everyone about medications and times for physical or other therapy.

You can add whatever and teach however you like. Keep in mind that your student still has to pass the test at the end of high school in order to move on to seek a higher education or certificate programs, get a job, or enter a vocational program. If your students are in special education classes because of language differences, you have the ability to teach in your language at home, provided your students are learning the same subjects taught in school.

This may be an opportunity for you to help your students progress very quickly with you or a tutor giving one-on-one attention they might not get in the class with other differently-abled students. You may be able to teach your students in such a way that it matches how their brains and bodies work. This may cause breakthroughs in progress you weren't expecting.

You're also going to have to overcome the anxiety of being in a completely different situation at home. Work with your students to help them understand what is going on and why they have to stay home.

You're going to be a caregiver for more hours than you're used to. You may have to hire someone to help you. You may also have to explain to your students why that person is wearing a mask and gloves in your household. Explain that this person is trying to protect everyone. What they are doing is required by the government. Help your students get over whatever fear or confusion they initially feel.

You may have to break things down into very small parts if you're working with students with different brains. Some neuroatypical students have sensory processing disorder, attention deficit disorder, autism spectrum disorder, or other brain differences. I have attention deficit disorder and need to change what I'm doing every 10-25 minutes. Children may need to switch subjects as little as every 10 minutes, depending on the subject. Or they may go into hyper-focus and fall down a rabbit hole, unable to stop studying a particular subject. You may want to give them a longer time if they're working on a subject they greatly enjoy, such as math, science, or reading.

Remember to deal with your frustration. You are going to have to eat correctly, exercise, and do all of the things you need to do to take care of yourself. If you're not getting enough sleep, you're going to have to try to get some extra help somehow. You are not a mutant alien from the planet Zenon who can do everything yourself without a break.

Even autistic students need contact with others. Neuroatypical students enjoy speaking to people who are also neuroatypical. Make sure your students can contact classmates or friends. This is a good time for your students to join online groups of people that like the things they enjoy, like science, magic tricks, or board gaming.

This may be time to start something new, like learning how to play something (with earphones involved), like electronic keyboards or drums. Make absolutely certain that your child has a rule about the earphones. You don't want the neighbors upset.

Many differently-abled students are extremely self-directed. You may be able to use the Khan Academy, YouTube videos, school in a box, or an online school. Your students may push forward very quickly once there are no other students to distract them in the class, and that could have caused them to slow down a great deal. It may be that taking subjects they greatly enjoy causes them to learn faster. Use the fun subjects as anchors, or scatter them throughout the day to give your students something to look forward to. Go as quickly or slowly as your student needs. Don't be surprised to experience breakthroughs you don't expect because being dragged from class to class or the distraction of other students isn't there.

Expect meltdowns from yourself and the student. This is a very strange situation for everyone. **Give both of you time outs.** If your student is safe learning in a room, you can go to the other room and cry or beat up a pillow if you need to do it.

Keep in contact with other parents of students with this particular issue. This may become more difficult if you have a student with multiple diagnoses. These people are going through the same things that you are. It may take a load off your shoulders when you realize that there are other people walking through the same situation. If you can't find a message board, Facebook, Twitter, or Instagram group about a particular issue, make your own! You might want to schedule Skype or Zoom calls as part of your week to touch base with various parents. If you don't know any, try to contact the other parents in your students' classes.

Use Regulations To Your Advantage

Most local governments have some sort of government regulation that says they must educate differently-abled students. Find out exactly what accommodations your students have, and if you can access them. You should already know this because you should have some sort of a learning plan your school has given you. If you don't know, contact the school or your students' teachers. Join the aforementioned groups and find out what parents are doing to hack whatever it is their students need. Don't be afraid to ask for help.

Contact the manufacturers of whatever devices your students need now that you're at home and don't have access to them. If you have the money, you can buy them. You may be able to buy them used, but you're going to have to disinfect whatever you buy thoroughly. You may be able to contact the government or a society that will help pay for this accommodation. Community and religious organizations may be able to help you if you don't have the funds. You probably will only have to prove that you don't have the funds. This may also take so much time that you must use some sort of hack until your student is back to school again. Do what you have to do so that your student can get the best education possible.

You don't have to be reliant upon a physical calendar. If your student is having a tough morning or afternoon, you can quit classes and finish them up later or on a half-day on the weekend. If your student is working ahead, as many do without all of the distractions of the other students and one teacher being responsible for many, you can just take time off. You can also switch to having Wednesdays and either Saturdays or Sundays off.

Retain some sort of structure. If you need to blow off steam and watch a movie or have a dance party, then do that. But, that's a special time, and that can't be every day unless it is scheduled and part of your curriculum. Remember, your student actually has to keep up with what they have to do in school. If they're working ahead, encourage that. You may be able to get your student in a different class at a later time.

Don't be afraid to ask for help. You are not a superhuman. You may find a group of people who are going through the same things that you are. You may be stunned at the tips and hacks that you receive. You may find some sort of diet that causes your students to suddenly behave or function much better. You may find an accommodation that cost $5 that you thought would cost $500. There's no way to know until you join, ask, even just lurk and find out what the other parents are saying.

Explain to your students that you're using them as scientific experiments, determining what works best in the home environment. Your students may be very eager to learn or integrate something new that will help them. Or, they may be very resistant. Explain very carefully that you are trying to make everyone's life easier, better, and have them learn in a better way.

There may be an app for that. Visually impaired or dyslexic people can use apps to read books to them. Google Docs has an extension called Read Aloud. Google Chrome even has a font for dyslexics. There are online services that do the reverse, transcribing audio to text. Google Chrome has a voice to speech tool under Tools. So, your student does not have to type laboriously! You can record an instructor's voice and play it back while Google Chrome types it out word for word. If you are watching YouTube videos, many have closed captions on the bottom. You can ask instructors for transcripts if they are doing reverse teaching (flipped learning). Look up apps for the differently-abled. There are new ones invented every day!

Percentages

No one is operating at 100% in the current crisis. Allow yourself to be at 80%, 70%, 60%, 50%. Get through the next five minutes, and take it one day at a time. Take a day off several times a month to just relax and watch movies or sports, have a dance party, or whatever to relieve the stress for both yourself and your kids.

School in a Box

School, classroom, homeschool curriculum, or academy in a box is something that many companies offer. They send books and educational materials to the students for money. They are definitely not free, and shipping may be prohibitively expensive. However, some students just don't function well in an all-electronic environment. They are easily distractible, have trouble managing their time, or simply like having something physical to work with. Very young children may do well having something physical in front of them. Some parents have spotty or little internet where they live, so online classes become an exercise in frustration.

There are specialized curricula that may focus on what your child wants to learn in a way that is respectful toward a language, culture, ethnicity, or religion. For instance, people of Greek heritage may want to learn ancient Greek, the language, history, and old stories. People of African, Asian, or Latin descent may prefer materials specific to them. Tracking what students are reading as well as covering a wide variety of materials is very easy with school in a box.

Some parents, having done everything literally by the book, do not understand the electronic educational offerings out there, and have no idea how to help their children with the material. Most online educational content is what we call **reverse teaching** or **flipped classroom**. A teacher teaches for five to twenty minutes or less, usually in a video or audio format, then the student has to do something in order to prove that the student has learned the material.

Remember, just because you haven't learned that way, doesn't mean that your student can or can't work that way. Don't pull the plug on electronic offerings or refuse to look into them unless you're certain they're not working. Remember, many online offerings are cutting edge with the newest in educational research about how students learn, and some are free.

How to Find Them

Most schools in a box are offered via online sellers. Essentially, you will receive a box for a year of school, such as kindergarten or sixth grade. The curriculum should include math, science, language studies, history, and anything else your child needs to know for that particular grade. Research what your district, city, state, province, or country requires for that grade before choosing a curriculum.

Get on homeschooling websites or join a homeschooling network to find the best educational resources, especially those with lower prices or free shipping, as long as they meet the criteria. There are hundreds of free printables from homeschooling sites that can be used as supplementary materials. Even if you're teaching from boxes, you'll still probably need a computer and a printer for handouts.

Never Write in the Books

For resale or having other kids in the family use the materials, *never write in the books*. Establish a system with cheap notebooks or legal pads to take notes and do homework. Many students find writing in legal pads much easier because it doesn't matter if they're right- or left-handed. They won't run into any sort of metal or plastic that can interfere with writing across the page. You can also use individual whiteboards or even the amazing new electronic pens that record what a student writes without paper. You can upload these notes using an app onto a computer or cell phone. This may save you a fortune in paper and protect the environment as well.

Each from-the-book assignment should be labeled with the student's name, the name of the book, page number, and the date. You can use separate notebooks or legal pads for separate books or subjects, or simply label each page by book and page number. You can use binder systems by subject as well. There are legal-sized plastic paper protectors and binders available online. You can scan the notes or take pictures of them on a cell phone and put the scans or pictures in an online folder. Do this to keep a record of what each student has done. You may need to do this for your school district to prove your student is being successfully homeschooled.

When you're done with the books, they can go to the next child in the family or group, or may be sold to another family that is homeschooling their children. With drop shipping, you can send books anywhere in the world. However, shipping heavy things like books can get expensive, so if you're selling them, include shipping in the price.

Homeschooling Networks

You may also be able to buy used resources from other parents in a homeschooling network. There are numerous websites with printables and much more. Homeschooling networks of people in your district or surrounding area may provide friends and study partners.

Parents may even be able to trade off teaching, especially since people are good at different things. For instance, someone in your network may teach your child woodworking, and you may teach your neighbor's children gardening. Until distancing restrictions ease, use Zoom or Skype calls to teach each other's students your skills. Take advantage of the learning opportunities all around you.

Socialization and the Community

Socialization is very important for kids. So are hobbies. Combine both. For now, make sure your children are able to communicate with friends via Zoom, Skype, or other free online communication tools. Perhaps you and your students can grow food for home or the local food bank.

Later on, when social distancing has been lifted, your children may want to participate in soccer, learn to play an instrument, or learn ceramics. There may be social or religious groups that have kids' groups. There may be community gardens or volunteer activities as well, such as gathering canned food for the local food bank. Be sure that the kids do not have too many activities, and that there is proper supervision. Overscheduling exhausts everyone!

Sensory Processing, ADD, Learning, and Other Differences

Some kids have genetic, mental, learning, sensory processing, and other differences. Many people with ADD use something called the Pomodoro method. Pomodoro is Italian for "tomato." This method uses a timer that rings out every 10 to 25 minutes. Then there is a 5 to 10-minute break to use the restroom, get a glass of water, or do a short chore. Then the students go back to what they were doing, or switch subjects. Most kids and adults over age 5 can benefit from this method. Add a minute per age of the student is the general rule. Generally speaking, high schoolers or even some tweens can do a full 25 minutes.

Or, your children may be hyperfocused, working in blocks of two hours on a particular subject. As long as all of the subjects are completed in the end, and the very important building block subjects such as math are not skipped, it's a good idea for the child to figure out the best schedule.

Learning Styles

Everyone's brain is different. People have different learning styles. Some people learn better by video, audio, visually, or by taking notes. My personal learning style is to read or study something, take extensive notes, highlight my notes, use icons in my notes, and then go back over them before I take some sort of test or have to do a project. One of the joys of learning at home is that each individual person can learn at their own pace in their own way.

If there are physical differences such as blindness, hearing loss, or sensory processing differences, work with specialists in that field to figure out what is best for each student in each particular case. There are many YouTube videos or websites you can use to get more information and determine the best way to go about educating your children.

Languages

Bilingual schooling is wonderful because it allows students to learn in different ways. There has been a lot of research that says that bilingual or multilingual students are able to learn a wide variety of subjects more easily because their brains have made different connections. It is of enormous benefit to teach students languages, the earlier, the better. If you have an infant, you can have someone read to your infant in a different language. Later on, they will be able to make sounds in that language more easily.

No matter what language is spoken in the home, it's a good idea to learn at least one other language. In this age of globalization, your child can grow up able to work on virtual teams with people all over the world. Having at least one other language is vital for success. If you are living in another country as an expat, take advantage and be sure you and your children learn the language(s) while you are there. There are apps, YouTube videos, and many language textbooks available.

People with linguistic differences should be able to teach their children in their home language. However, you do have to be sure that your students are fluent in whatever language the final examination is given. In the United States, the SAT and most high school equivalency exams are in English. For instance, if the language spoken in the home is Spanish with the equivalency exam at your school district given in English, make sure your kids are learning both Spanish and English so they are able to take the test. Don't wait until the year before the exam for them to learn English.

Required Reading Lists

There are required reading lists for students. Find the exact lists for each grade for the school district or country your child is required to learn. You don't have to buy every single one of those books. There are physical libraries that connect with online libraries using apps such as Libby and Overdrive. There are thousands of free books on Amazon's Kindle program which can be downloaded as an app to a smartphone, tablet, or computer.

Look for free books before you start purchasing books. Many required reading lists have books that were published centuries ago and should be free or available at a local or online library. Amazon has its Kindle reader app and a program called Kindle Unlimited. For about $10 a month you can read ten books in that program. There are thousands of books in Kindle Unlimited for you to choose from. Project Gutenberg has thousands of free books in the public domain you can download. If your students really want a physical book, look for them online on Amazon or the booksellers, or download and print the books from Project Gutenberg.

Hands-On Learning and Supervision

Some schools in a box are fascinating and exciting, with things like chemistry and building kits in them. You should definitely look into these whether you're learning electronically or not because there is no substitute for hands-on experience. However, things like scientific experimentation should be carefully supervised and should include non-toxic materials. You don't want to blow up your desk! Young children learn through play, music, and stories, so see if there are any of these materials available for kids at your local library, bookstore, or online.

Current Textbooks

Books have a writing—editing—printing cycle that can take years. Scientific understanding, even understanding of history and archaeology, changes over time. The only book from 1968 you can use is a math book, but with the "new math," I wouldn't risk it. Advances in science and technology change our understanding of the world all the time. You must get books that are as close to the current year as you can, or supplement the work with online resources.

For example, space travel is advancing with the beginning of private companies joining the space race. The latest rocket, satellite, or landing is not going to be in a book published even two years ago. You or your students have to dig deeper in order to get current facts. If you're learning or teaching kindergarten through approximately the fourth grade, there is nothing wrong with using older textbooks as long as the books are relatively new. You would be pushing it if they're over a decade old.

Hybrid Program

There is a program called the Robinson Curriculum that does not use paper textbooks. The curriculum is sent electronically to the parents, and parents print what they desire. So, you will need to have a printer or be able to use a local printer or copy store. The entire program is, as of this writing, $195 for K-12. This enables you to work without paying for expensive textbooks. There are other hybrid programs out there, many of them in a particular subject.

Equivalency Tests

Your child will need supplemental materials in order to pass whatever equivalency test there is to prove the child has learned enough in the required subjects to go to a university. Remember that the student has to take the test to join the military and for many jobs. Also, you may or may not be able to opt out of mandatory testing for your students. Once the lockdown has ended, if you want to continue to homeschool your kids you may have to take them to the local school to be tested a few times a year, depending on the school district or region.

Shipping

Remember that shipping can get expensive, especially with heavy items like books. You're also going to need to look ahead for when you're nearly finished with your box so you can find and order the next one and have it shipped to you. If you are an American living overseas and you are not in the military, make friends with military people! They may allow you to ship things to their APO (military) address more cheaply. Many other countries have similar low-cost shipping addresses for their soldiers or diplomatic personnel. Some online booksellers have discounted or free shipping on bulk items. Check out a variety of online educational booksellers; you may be able to rent textbooks if your kids do not write in them, or to rent them electronically.

Lowered Costs and Building Blocks

At-home students don't have to pay school fees or uniforms. These savings alone may tip the scales toward school in a box. If you have the funds and are able to have things shipped to you in a way that doesn't break your budget, then carefully research schools in a box. You do NOT want to have a student ready to take the high school equivalency exam and find out your child missed something important in the sixth grade.

Skills build on other skills. For example, missing algebra means a student cannot learn geometry and trigonometry. Students cannot skip courses because they do not like them or because they're inconvenient. This is still school. You can, however, help your students hack into finding a way of learning something that is interesting and fits learning styles. For instance, a student may learn geometry by figuring out real-world problems such as how to increase the number of parking spaces in a parking lot.

Time of Day

You may find that taking courses at certain times of the day is better for your students. For instance, many homeschoolers attack math first because it's such a building block. They get that out of the way, then "rest" by reading something from the required reading list. Many high school students like doing things late at night when they feel more awake, so they may get up at noon and take their school work during the afternoon or early evening. This schedule is supported by studies that say teens are more nocturnal.

School in a box allows your kids to learn whenever and wherever is best. Your kids can just take the book along with a notebook and a pencil or pen, and learn while waiting to see the dentist. Some students only want to learn in absolute silence, so if your student's little brother is playing the same ten notes on the violin for hours every day, you might want to have the older kids learn at night or early in the morning when their brother is asleep.

Truancy Laws

Once the lockdown lifts, if you want to continue using your school in a box, be careful when leaving the house because **truancy** (being out of school) is against the law in most places. There are laws in most countries about students having to physically be in school, and about students being out and about during the day alone. Many districts require that you have some sort of permission to be homeschooling. Some do not. Some require that a teacher looks over the students' work once a month or quarter. Be sure you find out about and follow the regulations for your district. If you need some sort of letter from your district allowing you to homeschool, students should have that paperwork with them when you leave the house. Be careful where your students are during school hours.

Time Off

Many parents find this incredibly freeing and respectful to family time to have their students working from school in a box. Once the lockdown lifts, they can take their kids with them on many adventures. Box schooling means that your students can go to school anywhere, work ahead, and take more time off during holidays or for trips. Just be sure to have a parent or guardian with your kids if the local schools are still in session!

Remember that the ultimate goal is to pass whatever test there is to prove that your child passed a certain grade, or the many high school tests like the state exams or GED in the United States. School in a box is an efficient way to do this. A student can work at one's own pace, speeding up, slowing down, putting materials aside when frustration becomes too great and going back to them later. Also, books can be supplemented with online materials, so a student can check out the cutting edge, leap ahead, explore interests, and won't have to lag behind other students even if they are reading older books.

Learning from home means your students don't have to waste time running back and forth in between classes going to their lockers and all those other things that students have to do during the school day. Many students work so quickly and efficiently that they are able to take their high school equivalency exams years before other students.

The students may also be able to attend college courses for high school credit, either online or physically, through Advanced Preparation (AP) or other courses. This saves a lot of money and time. Many students attend a local community college to attain their basic credits before moving to a regular university or even begin their university programs at a young age. You can hack your kids' education to the point the kids skip years of school! Many parents who homeschool their kids have had this experience. Keep this in mind when you decide what to do after the lockdown. Also, you could switch from online school to school in a box and back, or use one method with one kid and a different one with another, depending on age and circumstances. Homeschooling offers many choices!

Alternate Academics

Tired of books and worksheets? So are your kids! There are so many other things out there that kids can be doing that can also be counted as learning.

Chores

Build simple chores into your daily schedule. Make sure your kids make their beds. Your kids can put the laundry in the laundry basket. Teach them how to sort laundry and check the pockets. Decide on morning, afternoon, and before-dinner chores. As any parent knows, keeping the house clean is a constant battle. Even young kids can learn how to spray and wipe down door handles, light switches, desktops, and the like.

Take the time to figure out where everything in the house needs to go, even marking it out with washi (nonstick) tape. Several times during the day, with young kids, you can play clean-up music and make sure everything is in its box, bin, hook, or other place.

Exercise

This is a great time for kids to learn yoga, tai chi, calisthenics, dance, and/or martial arts. It burns off some of that excess energy they have and focuses them throughout the day. If it is possible for them to go outside wearing masks and maintain social distancing, you may be able to walk a trail or do something else to be in the sunshine. This will be extremely difficult in urban areas. Remember that they cannot touch metal outside, so taking them to a playground is a very bad idea at the moment.

Academic Tools

There are flashcards for every subject out there. Students can journal about any subject. Start with math in the morning, and include language arts and second language learning at some point during the day.

Kids can do brain puzzles like Sudoku, write in a journal, play strategy games like chess, or go through a study guide. Kids can record what they are doing, such as a play, blog, vlog, or other academic projects with a cell phone or screen capture software on computers. You can ban electronics (unless they're specifically recording something academic) during specific times when kids are using non-computerized or book tools. Teachers Pay Teachers is a great starting place to find games, projects, and more (including more worksheets). They do cost money, but you get real academic items you can use or print.

Manipulatives (physical objects used for learning) are fantastic tools like magnetic word packs used to make stories and various colored shapes used to make puzzles. Even measuring cups and spoons can be used to teach both cooking and math. You can use colored craft paper to teach origami. Look online for plenty of manipulatives, books, and lessons centered around them.

Tip: If you want to reuse coloring pages, math sheets, or anything else, laminate them or slide the sheet into simple plastic sheet protectors. Buy whiteboard pens with erasers in a variety of colors. The kids can reuse the sheets, so you don't have to reprint for multiple kids. You can also print or make your flashcards and laminate them or put them in plastic sleeves so kids can write on them, such as math flashcards.

Tip: Some kids hate coloring, so buy the "dabbers" used to color in Bingo cards for things they have to color in. Bingo is also a great game to play with your kids. You can create your cards that use words, pictures, or icons instead of numbers. This is a great way to teach vocabulary words.

Creative Play

Students can build Lego towers, construct elaborate marble slides or domino runs, draw, paint, learn new dance steps, play the recorder or keyboard, read academic magazines, make crafts like string bracelets or beadwork, and so much more. The idea is to have them engage their brains in ways that feel like play to them, but still make all sorts of connections in the brain over time. You may want to dust off the hobbies you put aside when you had kids and share them.

Cooking and Baking

Cooking simple meals is something children may want to learn anyway. Have fun cracking eggs together in a bowl or whatever else you do to help prepare for breakfast. Involve them in planning recipes for meals and snacks. Meal planning and making meals is important for kids to learn. Older kids can learn about shopping lists, budgeting, and how to find and order food online for the lowest cost. This is a great time to teach your kids about nutrition, how to get everything the body needs during the day.

Quiet Time

Parents and children both desperately need quiet time. This is time for reading, puzzles, and naps for the younger ones. This is a great time for older kids to read something from their required reading lists.

Electronic Study

Other than ebooks and etextbooks, this is a great time to play electronic educational games and apps, and watch educational shows like *Reading Rainbow*, *Between the Lions,* and many others. There are plenty of documentaries for older kids, but make sure the content is appropriate. **Starfall** has all sorts of content, like books, movies, and games for kids from kindergarten through the third grade. **Scholastic** has all sorts of content. So does National Geographic. Be sure you know what your kids are doing online. Lots of resources are free during the coronavirus lockdown. One preschool has a useful article about tools at www.cadence-academy.com/learning-tools-for-kids. You can find hundreds of articles out there about resources. Choose by the ages and grades of your kids, and explore!

Games

There are dozens of games that are fun and strategic at the same time, from Uno to Sushi Go. Older kids love games like Catan and Stratego. A simple Parcheesi game can make the entire family happy.

Note: This section is also found in the supplies list in this book.

Board Games
- Board games teach numbers, letters, shapes, and strategic thinking.
- Toddlers can learn rules and will learn games for older kids faster than you think. If you want to play more adult games, reserve those for when toddlers go to sleep.
- Take your time building a game library. Start with cheaper card games like Uno and save the expensive ones for when you can afford them. If you have the funds, buy them all!

- WATCH OUT FOR CHOKING HAZARDS. Toddlers will eat small pieces like marbles or put them in their noses or ears. Watch your little ones at all times!

Young kids: Candyland, Chutes and Ladders, Sleeping Queens, Go Fish, Go Fish Alphabet, Gobblet Gobblers, Zingo, Ruckus, Hoot Owl Hoot, Richard Scarry's Busytown, Robot Turtles, Feed the Kitty, Stack Up!

Elementary: Uno, Junior Skip-Bo, Skip-Bo, Parcheesi, Checkers, Sleeping Queens, Outfoxed, Sushi Go, Zingo, Tsuro, Rat-A-Tat-Cat, Spot It! Jr. Animals, Spot It!, Go Fish, Ticket to Ride First Journey, Ticket to Ride, My First Carcassonne, Qwirkle, dominoes, Labyrinth, Dixit, Otrio, Yahtzee, Jenga, Blokus, Taco Cat Goat Cheese Pizza, Tenzi, Q-bitz

Older Elementary/Middle School: Clue, Monopoly, Chess, backgammon, Rummikub. Carcassonne, Sequence, Catan Junior

High School and Up: Catan, Risk, Legendary, Takenoko, Steampunk Rally, Quantum, Terraforming Mars, Quadropolis, Five Tribes, Codenames, Apples to Apples, Mombasa, Orleans, Runewars, StarCraft, Falling Sky

This is just a starter list. There are many games out there. Check online gaming (and parenting) boards, videos, and sites to find out which ones gamers and parents rate highly. New ones are being invented all the time!

Project: Why don't you have your students invent their own games? Kids can make action, dance, dice, card, or board games themselves.

To make a card game, get some heavy construction paper and trace out card outlines. Kids can make flashcards, icon cards, any kind of card they want. Laminate them or use clear glue and plastic sleeves to cover them. Let them make their own rules, then have them write them down. Or, have them teach you how to play and write the rules down yourself.

To create a board game, you need a square or rectangle of cardboard covered with contact or construction paper. Your board can be a magical kingdom, an island, a spaceship, whatever you want! You can draw on your board, or if you have a printer, print out an image or images you copy or design.

You can make game pieces out of plastic toys, paper tubes, egg cartons, or plastic bottles, cut out or fold origami ones, make them from play dough, or order online from someplace like Etsy. You can also buy something called Inkjet Shrink Film; use this if you have both an inkjet printer and an oven at home. To use, find an image you want to use, double its size, print it out on the inkjet printer, and bake according to the directions.

Look up "DIY game pieces" or "how to make custom game pieces" online or on YouTube to make them out of dough or other materials. That's how lots of real-life games got started!

Behavioral Chart

This can be a simple piece of paper with smiley, so-so, and frowny face icons, or a stoplight of red, yellow, and green for each kid. Use magnets, stickers, or simple clothespins to let your kids know when they are doing well or badly. Bad behavior means no electronic time or time out on a chair. Good behavior means praise, more electronic time, or special time like baking the cookies they love. Teach children about emotions, and that they have to use their words like, "I feel ______."

You can get more complex with stickers and stars. A chore chart is a must-have to teach how to do chores—and persistence to get them done. Or, chores and good behavior can buy counters. You can make these out of wood, plastic, superhero magnets, or even colored dice. A certain number of magnets, dice, or stickers can buy electronic time, cooking a favorite treat or meal, getting a new book, more time playing their instrument, whatever they like. Make sure the rewards are clear and are not arbitrary or onerous. If kids want to trade, make sure they do not bully or coerce each other. This is a great time to teach negotiation skills, such as when one kid wants to trade extra electronics time stickers for some special snack stars.

Chore Chart

This can be simple (one chart for everyone) or complex (one chart for each person). You can find them online. Print them, order one online, or make your own. Use icons or pictures and color to make your chart the way you like it. Laminate them or slip them into plastic sleeves. Use stickers or write on the sleeves with erasable board pens. Or, use magnetic tape on the back so you can use colored magnets.

Note: There is a step-by-step process to make all three of these charts yourself in this book. They make great home projects!

More About Teaching

Aspects of Teaching

There are many aspects of teaching, including organization, lesson planning, and classroom management, to make sure your students are getting all of the information they need in order to pass the final test at the end of their educational career or in order to pass high school. You cannot learn every single subject in enormous detail. You may be learning alongside your students! You may have to hire tutors, use specialized textbooks, learn how to use computer programs, work with other parents, take the class with your kids, or even use virtual reality programs to teach those subjects. And that is okay! Professional teachers cannot know everything about every subject, either.

Teaching For Different Parts of the Brain

Teachers teach to various parts of the brain. The way that memory works in the human brain is that things are recorded and put into short-term memory. Then, if those things are important enough, they are filed away in the brain's long-term memory. In order to enable students to remember what they learned when it's time for them to use the skill or to be tested on it, it is best if information is filed in the brain in more than one area.

The way to do that is to use systems like color-coding, different fonts, highlighting, and icons. Some students go through their textbooks and highlight the most important sentence in the paragraph, then use a different color to highlight supporting facts. In order to pass a test, students just have to remember the coloring system that they used in order to find where everything is filed in the brain. Some use icon notes, so the icon triggers the brain to remember what the student wrote in the notes. Some kids use songs to remember data. The more "triggers" for this data, the easier it is for the students to recall the information later.

Teaching For Different Learning Styles

There are so many aspects of teaching. One of them is making sure that you're teaching clearly. Another is teaching to various parts of the brain. The left brain is analytic, and the right brain is creative. Teach to both sides of the brain by having students analyze what they have learned, and explain it in creative ways. To integrate the analytical left brain and the creative right brain, students can create wonderful notes based on icons or other graphics. Learn more about this style of note-taking at www.doodlenotes.com.

Students learn in several different ways, including visual (sight), auditory (sound), and kinesthetic (movement). For instance, one student may see and listen to an instructor, but also need to take extensive notes and highlight them. Some students have to be moving to learn; schools are not set up to handle these students. Some students learn through music, drawing, sports, and interpersonal relationships. For instance, some students pair a particular song or type of music with studying a particular subject. They memorize long lists of things like elements or presidents with rap rhymes. Those are your musical learners. Some type with one hand while scribbling with the other hand. Find out how your learner learns by asking questions and observing them.

Note: With a student who is always moving, one trick is to tie a jump rope to the bottom of their chair so they can kick it. Let them stand while learning or rotate where they learn (bedroom, couch, kitchen table). Give these students frequent activity, sports, or dance breaks.

Note: Teachers use all three modalities to promote learning. Then they think about how to make a backup plan for each modality for each part of a lesson. Now think if you are a teacher for 20, 30, 45, or more students like you would if you were in many of the school systems around the world. Believe it or not, some school systems have 70 children in a class. Try tailoring an education to the learning styles of all the students in a large classroom! This is why teachers keep advocating for smaller class sizes.

Different Classwork

Now you can see how hacking your kids' education is useful! You can tailor each method of learning to each student. You can learn how to teach different modalities like voice for the auditory learner, visuals that pop for visual learners, and why kinesthetic learners love taking notes and doodling with colored pencils. Teachers can also tailor how the students prove that they have learned something using technology and all three methods of learning.

I teach in as many ways as possible. I also assign classwork or homework that can be delivered in several ways. Your kids may do videos, act out plays, put together a diorama, or create a podcast. Your students may study via videos, podcasts, and even need to see or create their own infographics. These assignments or self-directed classwork items can be put together into a portfolio. Teachers and tutors love portfolios. They are excellent snapshots of what students can do. It also lets students learn and produce work in their best learning modalities.

Note: You do NOT have to do what the school does, or in the way they do it. As long as your students get to the same place in learning. Doing things differently while teaching the same subjects is like you and your kids taking the train to the same station as other students. It may be a faster or slower train or bus, but they all go to the same stop.

Written tests are not the only way to check for comprehension! You can ask your students questions about what they have learned, and they can answer verbally, write answers, draw, or even act out the answers. For instance, students may do videos on their phones about the practices of people that lived thousands of years ago in your area. They can create a newspaper or newsletter based on the goings-on in a small community in ancient times. They can create a detailed report on what these people ate, their ceremonies, and many more things. They can put on plays.

Your students can band with other students to make podcasts without physically having to be in the same room with someone else. Students may create a newsletter, or learn from other students' podcasts. Kids can even record lessons or create materials such as infographics for next year's students to use! Your school website may have an area to upload projects like this. If they don't, ask them to make one!

Technology and Classwork

Classwork like podcasts and videos are great ways for students to learn to use new skills that are needed in the current technological environment. You can put together very good podcasts and videos nearly free if you have an iPhone. Or, you can put together an entire video set with lighting, a so-called green or white screen, and much more. Many people are using corners of their apartments, closets, and other household areas to shoot videos. You can learn how to do this using free or low-cost videos and courses on Udemy, YouTube, and more.

Let students do projects that cross different subjects in ways you can't do in a regular school environment. For instance, you can talk about the art, history, language, and culture of specific historical events. History isn't just names and dates; that's actually a very poor way to teach history. You can also teach things such as economics and science while you're teaching about a time period like the industrial revolution in Europe. This time period affected economics, health, the environment, and many more things.

You can also teach ancient history by having your students play a game where they learn how to run a castle. Food, clothing, shelter, and the so-called domestic arts were paramount at that time. Tasks took many hours. For instance, living in a castle involved animal husbandry, metalworking, material arts, stoneworking, and far more. You can teach about the economics of crafting. You can even have your students form groups with other classmates and figure out how they would run their own castle. For older students, you can have them create or program a game or simulation about running a castle. They may even make money selling the game! You have far more leeway to have your students do interesting projects that the regular school system would never have time to allow because having so many students and the constant testing takes away many hours of instruction.

This is also a great way to teach your students about your beliefs. If you want your students to learn to be environmentally friendly, have your students research why the Industrial Revolution was so devastating to the environment. Teach them critical thinking by having them point out good points of this time period, such as people were able to do a lot more work in far less time. You can deliver a far more well-rounded viewpoint than just what a textbook gives. The real world is far more nuanced. You can cross disciplines to your heart's content. That's part of the point of homeschooling.

See what educational games and software are out there. There are many free or low-cost courses online for older students to dig more deeply into the subjects that interest them, such as *Crash Course* or *SciShow*.

Your job is spark excitement. The single best thing you can do is to teach your students to be lifelong learners. Learning does not stop when people graduate. Technology constantly changes. The vast amounts of data that have been collected in just the last two years are astonishing. Students need to learn how to handle massive changes and vast amounts of information in very short periods of time.

Virtual Reality

Virtual reality will change how students learn. This technology will allow you to send your children to the bottom of the ocean, to other planets, to see the universe. This is an astonishing, amazing technology. As virtual reality develops better educational software and virtual worlds, students can learn all sorts of skills and be able to see and do things that they never had access to before, such as windsurfing, jogging on a beautiful beach, or learning tai chi from a master from home. You can visit ancient Rome or a space station. More space stations are going to be built, some private and some public. In the coming decades, that may be where your students will work! We have no idea what the future holds. But now you can investigate virtual reality educational programs. They will get better and better over time.

Low-income families may not have access to virtual reality. Parents can speak to virtual reality manufacturers and virtual educational game designers and see if their students can be testers.

Students should learn coding, 3D modeling, storytelling, and game design if they want to be able to design their own virtual games or even virtual educational environments. We don't know what the reality will be in the future. We do know that students are going to have to learn a vast number of things in a very short amount of time. Immersing themselves in a virtual world can allow them to learn on a more physical level what it is they need to know.

Have your students learn the virtual world more thoroughly. If you can, have your students learn to program virtual reality environments, 3D modeling, and whatever else can be used to create a virtual reality environment. Remember that your students have the capacity to learn amazing things. They will be able to get jobs in fields that do not exist presently.

Your students may be able to participate in all sorts of trials and studies of these new products or to learn how to design them themselves. They may be able to design their virtual educational games, maybe even be able to sell them. Remember, you want your students to learn a wide variety of skills. Technology is a STEAM (science, technology, engineering, art, and math) skill!

Differences

Every student is different. Some will want to learn alone in a room, others in a busy family room. Some students will have an overwhelming urge to get up and move around and not want to sit in front of the computer at all. The problem for all educators is differentiating among the students. Three children from the same family will have vastly different attitudes toward education, overall outlook, perceptions, interpersonal relationships, and their own balance among everything. Teachers desire the student who is able to study large amounts of material in a short amount of time because this current world requires students to sift through large amounts of data. But students also need to be able to play, laugh, and enjoy the world around them.

If your students have learning differences, band with other parents and students with the same difficulties, and work together to come up with solutions. Make sure these students get more physical activity and brain resting time and are able to work in such a way where they won't distract each other. Read every book, article, and more that you can find from legitimate researchers in that area. People find out that old research is completely invalid, or is missing key factors. New research is able to come up with new solutions that previous research failed to find.

You have no idea what is going to work with your student until you try it. Use your scientific curiosity to discover how your student works best; what form of study, playtimes, and what form of learning works best for them. Your students may want to do all the schoolwork in one long block, and another cycle through in 25-minute increments. This is not supposed to be a form of psychological torture. This is supposed to be learning how your student thinks and absorbs information, and how to put in play and enjoyable projects to make learning fun.

Remember also that your student is going to change over time. What is true today will not be true next week, next month, next year. One of the worst things you can do as a teacher is to get into the "I know exactly how my students work until the end of time" frame of mind. Your students' brains and bodies change. Body chemistry changes. Brain chemicals go up and down. There may be a time when the dopamine levels are very high and your student wants to do a tremendous amount of work, and times when the level is very low and your student needs to take a day off. Because you're hacking a child's education, and because you are not necessarily constrained to the Monday through Friday world, you may be able to give a child a day off on Wednesday and do a little more work on Thursday. This completely depends on what is going on in your lives. Learn to pivot with the changes.

Systems

Not everything is going to go perfectly. What will help is preparation, preparation, and more preparation. The idea is to have relaxed, open learning while still having your students have to prove what they have learned. You may want to design colorful worksheets. There are programs like Canva, BookBrush, and many more that can allow you to create books, workbooks, infographics and more. There are also many free templates to make your own worksheets and materials. There may be new incredible worksheet programs out there that you can use. That changes all the time. You never know what some software companies can put out. You will have to do some research on your own because these things change so rapidly.

Having a system is going to be extremely vital for you. Having a system will enable you to determine exactly where the students are, what your students need to do to progress, what subjects they have gotten ahead on and where they're behind, and more. Doing things at your own pace means that some students may be zooming past everyone else in their grade level in one area, but be very far behind in another. Don't worry about this. Different students learn at different rates. The point is that you know where your student is, and you can know what areas in which your student needs extra work.

This may sound very confusing, daunting, and overwhelming. Remember, you can get the help you need. You can take online courses on teaching and classroom management. You can learn all about visual, auditory, and kinesthetic learning online. You can learn about whatever brain differences your student may have.

You can learn about what activities work best with students at different ages. One of the main things you have to learn is that younger students work in different ways than older ones. Younger students love music, color, movement, and more. If you want to string together a rap song with the names of the presidents, prime ministers, or planets, go for it.

Older students are much more able to sit in front of a computer for hours and may have even more trouble regulating themselves than younger ones. The reason is that they may do a deep dive into certain subjects. You do want to encourage that when you're teaching and are hacking your child's education.

Immersive Learning

Part of the fun is if students can find a fascination, such as skateboarding, and immerse themselves in it. If a student becomes obsessed with skateboarding, they should learn everything from how the skateboards are made, to safety, to modeling new skateboards, to the physicality of the tricks, and much more. They can also learn everything including all the aspects of running a skateboard business. This could be making skateboards, teaching skateboarding, and tricks. They can learn the geometry of flying through the air, or what it would cost to build a skateboarding park in your area. Maybe your student can even work with the local community leaders to get funding to create a skatepark if there's none in your area. There are all sorts of things your student can learn about math, science, economics, history, athletics, and more from immersion in one subject.

There are all sorts of subjects that can be investigated and modeled this way. You don't want them to go so far down their obsession they don't do their work in other subjects. Be sure they're still progressing in other areas such as math, science, and history. Students could put some of it aside while they're doing a deep dive, but when they resurface, they're going to have to work on these things again.

The ultimate question is, what is it that you hope for your students to learn and understand? Everything from ancient history to current politics? Do you want them to understand the way the world and the universe work? Do you want them to articulate their position in a debate and be able to clearly explain what they think and why? The more you understand what you want your students to learn, then do, the easier it will be for you to teach them.

Some of this is really straightforward. With math, you're trying to have your students apply mathematical theorems and formulas to help them solve problems, preferably problems they see in their everyday lives. Why would you need to know, unless you are a train operator or running a train system, when two trains coming from opposite directions moving at certain rates will cross paths? It is better to teach solving a variety of problems that are in the real world. For instance, how do you get people and materials to remote areas of the world that are in trouble, such as having a famine, conflict, or epidemic? That's a very valuable question, and that can help people in a wide variety of careers. The train problem is more academic and less real. There are all sorts of brain teaser programs that postulate a lot of these problems. Just be very careful what you're doing is age-appropriate. Be sure to understand what your student can and can't do at a certain age.

Things that are beyond their current skill levels can be done if the students are built, bit by bit, up to that level. Once the student is at that level, then your student is better able to build and go to higher levels. Be absolutely certain that the student understands a level underneath in order to do the next step.

Build in a lot of review into teaching. This allows the students to go back over what they learned previously and build on it. For instance, you're going to teach young students words, sentences, sentence structure, and grammar. Then when they get a bit older, they need to know how to put together a paragraph with the topic sentence and supporting details. Then you're going to want to teach how to put those paragraphs together. Teach them to create and look for the topic sentence for each paragraph, making it much faster to write a book report or essay. Then teach them how to make an outline. Outlining can greatly decrease the time in which it takes for a student to write.

Older students should learn to write quickly, clearly, and concisely about topics that they may have never heard of or had an interest in. Students need to be able to do book reports to explain what is in a book and why it is relevant. Many school districts have required reading lists. Be certain that the material is not completely over your students' heads.

You may want to teach the history, language usage, and other things of a certain time to make sure that your students understand what is being said in literature from that time. When I learned Shakespeare, I learned a lot about Elizabethan England in order to understand Shakespeare's plays. I had to learn about Shakespeare's life, the Globe Theater, and learned from books that had the plays and sonnets on one side with a more modern translation on the other for me to understand the language. After a while, I was able to immerse myself in the time. I soon greatly enjoyed learning about Shakespeare's plays. The themes have very modern twists. There are movies, TV shows, and more modeled upon the plays. Immersive learning is superior learning!

Home School Regulations

Generally speaking, as long as you have your high school diploma, you can teach your children through high school. This depends on each district, city, state or province, or country. However, many parents feel overwhelmed with teaching. If you want to move past the information in this book, you can take courses on classroom management, teaching skills, teaching online, teaching special needs students, and much more online on sites like Udemy and Coursera. Udemy has free and low-cost courses. Coursera is free. Skillshare has many classes; you can do some courses for free, or sign up for them at a fee. At the time of this writing, Skillshare is $15 a month.

Teacher Certification

If you have the money and the time and you want to keep your kids at home longer, or even teach other people's kids, you can become a certified teacher yourself. If you want to teach in the United States, you can join the online certification program through ABCTE, the American Board for Certification of Teacher Excellence. This certificate is good for 15 US states at the time of this writing. It's about $1900, and you have to take two tests in a major city through a testing center. You can learn overseas. I used the Pearson center and learned in South Korea. **This is only if you want to become a certified teacher.** This is certainly not necessary to homeschool your kids.

Mission Statement, Values, and House Rules

This is designed to give your family something to sit down, agree on, and work towards. This should **not** be parents dictating to kids, but time for kids and parents to sit down and develop these things. This is a great project to do as a family unit!

Mission Statement

What is your family all about? Love, kindness, togetherness? Respect? Standards? Doing what is right rather than what is easy? Keeping things simple?

Example: Our family is kind, respectful, and listens to others. We believe we were put here on the planet to love each other as a family unit. We calmly speak our truth out loud. We think all people are the same all over the world. We work to make this world a better place with our strong hands and hearts.

Example: Our family is built on trust and love. We love, trust, and respect others. We are helpful and kind even when we want to be angry and selfish. We have strong feelings about the environment and our community.

Values

Make a list of values for the family. Some of them will be from your culture, your spiritual or religious background, and/or how you think responsible people should act in the world.

Example:
1. Be respectful.
2. Put your family first.
3. Listen to each other.

House Rules

Kids used to be at school and did not have to think about home rules. This makes it obvious what kids can and cannot do in the home. **Do not write too many rules. *Rules follow values.***

Example:
1. No yelling or screaming.

2. Keep your room clean.
3. Keep your hands to yourself.
4. Schoolwork is first before playtime.

Now, make your list using the outline below. Print it out or make a beautiful poster.

Our Mission Statement

Values

House Rules

Motivation

This is a situation that has never happened before worldwide. There have been epidemics before, even pandemics. But the entire world has never dealt with a severe problem that affected us all, that shut us down, isolated us, and has such far-reaching medical, governmental, economic, and social impacts. This will cause permanent changes in how we, as a planet, run things. Millions of people are and will be without jobs for possibly years to come. More and more people will work from home.

Over a billion parents are now home teaching their kids. Most have never had training in teaching. These parents often feel alone, cut off. Their kids are confused, anxious, and begging to go outside, to see their friends. Being trapped for months brings out the best and worst of human behavior, including that of anxious parents and confused kids with nowhere to go.

Percentages

In such an environment, **think in terms of percentages**. Do the best you can within the confines of that day, that block of time, that hour. Don't worry if you are operating at 70%, 60%, 50%. The best that most of us can do on our best days in this situation is 80%. Let the rest go.

Planning

Make a list of what has to be done in order of priority. Everyone must be fed and have enough to drink. That is Priority One. The next priority is **your relationships with each other**. This is a strange statement for an educator to make, but it is true. Love is an action. Respect, kindness, honesty, gentleness, trust, all of these are parts of love. Put them into your actions. If you are trapped in a house with each other, make boundaries, like you can't come into my room without permission or we use our inside voices. Try to eliminate stressful things like cooking three-course meals, unless cooking de-stresses you.

Balancing Education and Work

Balancing your kids' education and your work may be a delicate act that requires a LOT of planning. Kids need to see both their schedules and their parents' work times and understand exactly when that parent will come back from their work. Lop off your workspace, and make a rule the kids can't come in. **Set a timer** (add 5-10% for overflow and transitions) and then come in so the kids know that when *Read Between the Lions* or *Sesame Street* is over, you will come back in.

Chores

Next, make a list of chores. Doing these through the day and involving your kids will greatly cut down on stress. This is a fantastic time to teach your kids how to make the bed, how to make a sandwich, how to keep surfaces clean, and the like.

Contingency Planning

Make a list of what to do if X goes wrong. What if all the kids have a meltdown at the same time? What if we run out of Y? If you think things out, you can maneuver around or find fixes for problems before they arise.

Be Realistic

Be kind to yourself. **No one on the planet is operating at 100% right now.** Get over your special self and realize that **50%-80% is okay.** Get through the next minute, the next five minutes. Get through one day at a time. **If you feel like you are going to melt down, set the timer, put on a video for your kids, and go to your room to cry or beat up a pillow** for twenty minutes. During quiet time, take your own quiet time. **Make a "golden hour" of quiet time mandatory.** Everyone needs a break!

If you are at 10%, make a pretty princess or sports or movie or downtime day. Make your favorite foods, snuggle up under the covers, and watch stuff on television. Or, have a dancing, project, or play day, or whatever it is that de-stresses everyone. Do this twice a month or even once a week.

Talk to Other Parents

Start a book, movie, or parental support and venting group. **Talk to other parents.** You are not alone!

Stop the Crazy

Teaching from home can cause a sense of lethargy, anxiety, and exhaustion even though you're not running around outside the house doing a bunch of things. You may feel stuck, like a fly in amber. This can lead to students and parents with absolutely no motivation. The problem with free-floating anxiety is that it's exhausting, and it's not something you can put on some boxing gloves and fight.

The key here is physical exercise. Use it as a push to get your blood moving and brain working. I get out of bed and do my 22 minutes of high-intensity interval training every day, even though I have nowhere to go and nothing to do at the moment. This helps me deal with my anxiety and puts it in perspective. I push the anxiety, confusion, and lethargy out of my body using weights and kickboxing moves. Then I push forward to doing the things I need to get done today.

You stop the crazy by moving. Do things you can do in a small area if you are in a tiny apartment. Walk around in circles doing lunges and arm lifts. Listen to podcasts or dance to amazing music while you're working out. I dictate books while cleaning the house. I know you're emotionally exhausted, but if you exercise 4-5 times a week within 80 to 90% of your ideal heartbeats per minute for seven to twenty minutes, you can help your heart health, and find a way to focus your brain. Exercise is wonderfully focusing.

Take this as an opportunity to learn yoga, martial arts, or dance, something that can be done indoors. If you have enough room in your household, maybe your small kids can do some tumbling on a very thick yoga mat. I think it is very important for parents to get up early and do their exercise before the kids wake up. I know it's very tempting to sleep in for hours and hours. That free-flowing anxiety and the edge of depression makes everyone exhausted and a little crazy.

You need a schedule. Use the one from the school, one from a homeschooling website, or one you created yourself. If you have a job, make a work calendar. Put both calendars up so you can see what to do. There are several in this book for you to choose from.

Everyone needs things to do. Make a series of lists. Divide them into short and long tasks. Break down long tasks into short parts. I use a Pomodoro timer and do my longer tasks in 25-minute bursts and use 5-15 minute breaks to do the little tasks, like put the laundry in the washing machine or sweep one room.

Make a Kanban Board

A kanban board is a task board, monthly or even quarterly. You can order a board to be shipped to you. Or you can make an online or physical kanban board. You can also create one with a piece of cardboard or an old poster frame. Cover it with chalkboard or whiteboard contact paper, use washi tape around the outside, and hang it up. Rather than a calendar version, you can create a task version. Take little sticky notes and write down one task on each one. Break down a big task, like creating a podcast, from writing the first words to final upload, and stack them.

Whenever you do not know what to do next, just grab a little sticky note and do it. Put the done ones at the bottom of the board or in a bowl, can, or box to see what you have accomplished. Reward yourself with time off for a full bowl, box, or can! You can do the same thing with electronic to do list apps. Use the Pomodoro Method and do a mix of longer and shorter tasks throughout the day. Find some little or low-stress tasks you can weave into the big ones to de-stress.

Lists for Breaks

I have the Kindle reading app, and over time I've downloaded free and low-cost books, and they're sitting there, unread. Many of them are nonfiction on things that I need to know for my profession, such as blog writing or Facebook ads. I made a list of fiction titles and then nonfiction titles, and I read them on my breaks when my eyes start to cross after staring at a computer screen. I also made a list of Udemy courses that I have not currently taken. I can do those in short bursts, do a module from time to time. I can also work on making my small apartment look the way I want. These are things I'm salting into my regular day.

Break Days

You can have two break days in a different spot than weekends if you are at home, like Sundays and Wednesdays. I take Sundays to do anything I want, like lay in bed, read books, watch YouTube and Netflix, and play video games. Do whatever it is you need to do in order to clear out your brain to work well for the next few days.

Kid Motivation

Kids don't understand why they can't see their friends, why everyone is suddenly at home all the time. They don't understand why they're trapped indoors when there is sunshine outside. Social distancing makes no sense to a child. Children need to be held and loved. Wash your hands and hug your kids. Do things with them. With younger kids, sit on the floor and play with them when you can.

Let all your kids have free time for one or two hours a day to do what they want. Let them use the electronics. That's not bad parenting in this situation; it is sanity-saving. When they squabble, try to separate them out in various rooms with different activities. Have game nights. Watch silly things, dance around, laugh. Release the pressure through togetherness and laughter, and resting yourself if you can when your kids have their quiet time.

Texts, Phone Calls, Skype, and Zoom

Set up calls where kids can speak with their friends. Work with other parents to form a group for kids who are in the same grade to learn together using online study sessions. Use technology to help kids connect with their friends in a way that keeps social distancing but does make them feel connected. This isn't a reward; it's part of having happy, well-adjusted, social kids. Do the same thing yourself, like a book, TV show, or movie Zoom group for adults with your friends.

Organize The House

One of the biggest parental headaches is toys and other kid stuff. Put things in baskets, bins, trays, and cups, then label everything with words, icons, or have the kids draw colorful pictures. Use nonstick washi tape to mark out where everything goes for smaller items like a pen cup or earphones. Make a rule to have only one basket, bin, or box of toys or crafts out at a time, and everything goes back in before you pull out another one. This cuts down on clutter and prevents your stepping on a Lego piece or doll furniture at three in the morning.

Put school and craftwork in nested or stackable boxes. Keep it all on the same shelf or part of the house. Everything goes back in the bins after each project so you're not stepping on colored pencils and breaking them. Definitely have picking up time before lunch and dinner. Give cleaning and picking up fun music and use dance moves. If everything has its place, decluttering should be fast.

Mix Fun and Academics

Intersperse fun things with academics. Students need to learn things like art, music, and physical movement. Do projects the schools do not have time to do, like making glitter slime or playdough. That's science! There are many free YouTube videos that describe academic projects students can do.

Haters

You may have a student who absolutely hates school, or who finds school incredibly boring. This student may have trouble getting along with other students or prefers isolation to noise.

There are many reasons why a student can have these feelings. Some students have learning or physical differences, have moved around a lot, have been put in difficult situations like divorce or sudden moves, feel they have not been listened to, are gifted and talented, or are from another culture or language forced to go to school with people that are not of their culture and language. These students may need physical, psychological, and academic testing to determine the underlying causes. Some students need a special diet, proper exercise and rest, counseling, and possibly medication. Read the chapter on differently-abled students for more information.

There is one very clear way that might motivate them. Tell them that if they pass all of the parts of the equivalency test to get out of high school, they can take the test and graduate early. It doesn't matter if they're twelve or seventeen, but they have to pass all the parts of that test in order to graduate. Advanced Placement classes allow students to take college credits while in high school. If you explain that doing the work systematically gets it out of the way so they can enter a university, certificate, or vocational program, many students will do the work in exchange for their academic freedom.

Most school-hating students respond very positively to homeschooling because they want to get out of high school or even middle school. They may need tutors. They need scheduling tools to do self-directed learning. If they want to train for something that they can do as a job, have them research what they want to learn, such as coding. They can learn to code for free online at Free Code Camp. Udemy has many certificate programs. Help your students find something that they enjoy. They will grow, learn new skills, and improve over time.

Make sure they take art, music, and coding. Introverted people like things they can do alone like coding and playing the guitar. Extroverted people also exist and like other more social things. Don't force your students if they are in what I call an "angry bear" phase. The angry ones may disdain physical exercise, but martial arts, tai chi, or kickboxing may help work out frustration and anger.

Many students have started home businesses. Some have even developed multimillion-dollar companies! Have them brainstorm ideas to do something that costs little or no money to begin. This may occupy them when their classwork is done.

If your students want to work, they need to take small business courses like business accounting. With the advent of the 3D printer and online design tools, some students are running profitable businesses out of their homes. One person I know designed a game that he was able to sell on Kickstarter. Some people make toys or games to sell with their 3D printer. See the part in this book on creating your own games.

Occupational Surveys to Promote Motivation

You may also want to virtually take them to small business owners nearby, especially in the field they want to get into, in order to show them how to do it. This is a wonderful opportunity for them to learn about various businesses to find out what they want to do and how to get to what they want. Have them interview people by telephone and Skype about various jobs.

Sit down with your student and brainstorm interesting jobs in your area, then contact these people. First, create a list of questions that would be useful. You can go electronic, and make this a short survey on Google forms. Many people would be absolutely delighted to do this because they're sitting at home and would welcome something to do. Make your email extremely short explaining about the class and that you would request that they fill out this form.

Have them send a very polite email that says, "I'm working on a paper for my writing class. I would like to request 10 to 15 minutes of your time to ask you a few questions about your occupation." Many people have the time to help your students learn now. Create and link a Google Form for their convenience.

Think very carefully about people's privacy. Ask for a first name and occupation. Find out what these jobs entail, what education do people have in order to do them or what life experience, and what your student would need to do in order to have that type of job. What are the strengths and weaknesses of the job? What are the good and bad points? What skills or type of personality do you need to have in order to do the job? Make sure there's one spot at the bottom where the person can write anything they want, such as, "What do you think I should know if I'm thinking about this type of profession?" Google Forms will compile all the answers for you.

These surveys can be expanded into areas such as sports, news, game design, whatever it is you like. Your students can focus on the jobs they find the most interesting or try to find a cross-section of all the jobs in your area. This can also be expanded into other things, such as surveys of other students and how they are learning at home.

Whatever you do, make sure your student has to have an output based on this information. Your student can write a short paper on this particular topic, or even several papers. This is a great way to teach them how to compile information, figure out what is the most important information, and put it into a report. That is a skill that can help them for the rest of their lives.

A Day Off

If no one is motivated, give everyone a half or full day off. Check your calendar for holidays that you may not have thought to observe because you are stuck at home, or make up one! Then, start over the next day. Or give yourself a three-day weekend, especially if the kids are working ahead in their schoolwork. Why not? Part of the point of being at home is that you can do what you want!

Overbearing or Helicopter Parents

Overbearing parents try to live their lives all over again through their children. That never works. People have completely different skills, personalities, likes, and dislikes. You cannot choose what your children like or enjoy.

The children of overbearing parents either run when they are able to get free, or they subsume their hopes and dreams under someone else's hopes and dreams. Sometimes they have happy lives, but most do not. If you give up who you really are, you're generally not a happy person.

Helicopter parents hover over their kids, watching their every move, constantly criticizing them or passing out praise for extremely minor things. These parents have read too many books and watched too many movies and videos on how to parent. They have forgotten that people need to learn how to make their own choices, even at a younger age.

The best parents around me help their children make choices at an early age. In the morning, they approach their toddler, hold up two shirts appropriate to the weather and climate, and say, "Do you want the red one or the blue one?" At first, you're going to have to limit your child's choices because they're too young to understand things like they can't wear their short-sleeved shirt when it is cold outside. The idea is to allow more and more choices, so by the time a young person is a tween, they are able to make more and more decisions. Being a teenager in today's world involves making life choices with sometimes severe consequences.

Sometimes this is very difficult. There may be a child who made a lot of terrible decisions, or maybe the parents made terrible decisions when younger and are trying to prevent their offspring from doing the same thing. They forget that everyone learns by making mistakes.

Some parents have to make most of their children's decisions even when their children become adults, such as with people with certain disorders like fetal alcohol syndrome. Some people's brains just can't make healthy decisions.

The problem with being a helicopter or overbearing parent is that the person never grows up to make healthy decisions. A number of us have friends who never quite grew up. They simply don't have the maturity to make decisions. I am not talking about people with brain differences, but those who never learned from their parents how to make the best decisions for themselves.

For example, my parents talked about money very briefly, and then that was it. I didn't know how to shop, find deals, clip coupons, or do anything that could have helped me save money. They showed me a checkbook and took a few minutes on how to balance it, and that was it. I didn't know about credit, lending, loans, or any of the other things I should have understood in order to make financial decisions. I was out on my own, missing a lot of the information I needed in order to function. Of course, I eventually learned money management as an adult.

Parents have the job of teaching life skills. Pretend you are teaching your kids a life skills class. Being an adult is extremely difficult with the large number of decisions that need to be made. If you prevent your child from making decisions for themselves and stifle their creativity, they do not learn about what they like and don't like. Their sense of curiosity and wonder is eventually destroyed.

Do not relive your childhood using your child, such as assuming they love math, sports, chess, or the oboe when you are the one who loves these things. Listen to your child. Find out what they want, need, and desire. If you find yourself trying to relive your childhood (this is a common impulse), please close your mouth and listen. Parents who try to change their kids into little copies of themselves miss many beautiful moments where their child tells them important things. They miss them because they are busy running roughshod with what they think their child should be doing. I know they think they are being protective. But, overprotective parents often leave their children unable to make healthy decisions for themselves.

Overbearing and overprotective parents often have no idea what their offspring's strengths and weaknesses are. They often do the opposite, pushing them to excel at their weaknesses and ignoring their strengths. You can't teach a blunt child to be a diplomat or one who hates art to make beautiful ceramics. If you do, that child will end up being angry and resentful for being forced to live a life that they have no intention of living. And that would be a sad fate I know you don't want for your child.

That doesn't mean that if your offspring whines about having to take math that you pull them out of it. Math is required in order to graduate from high school. Just don't push your child into being a nuclear physicist on the first day. You may be able to make an end run about the problem if you know your child well enough. For instance, you can teach your child about astronomy, see them fall in love with the stars, and help them learn that there is math involved in orbital mechanics. They may find some hook, some way to love a subject they used to hate if you are able to catch their wonder and imagination.

Those are the keys, wonder and imagination. Curiosity. A joy of learning. Overprotective and helicopter parents and too rigid schooling drive away the joy out of nearly everything. They force a child to focus on things they're not remotely interested in, demand perfection when their child is growing and learning, and completely flip out when the child makes a mistake. Mistakes are part of learning. You can't learn without them.

Allowing your offspring to hack an education means you take your hands off the wheel, let them direct the boat. You may be very surprised at how much they are willing to excel when wonder and curiosity are reignited. Most of all, if your child is afraid of you, terrified of making a mistake, you might want to look at your parenting. Many people believe they have a little adult, not a child. Children are not small adults and should not be expected to be that way. They need play and time to pursue their own interests. That doesn't mean you have to treat your child like a baby. It does mean that if you take away all the fun in life, your child is probably going to be miserable. I don't think anyone actually wants a miserable child.

Online Predators

There are people who prey on the vulnerable. They may be psychotic, sociopathic, or pedophiles. Or, people may have other pathologies such as being highly critical and perfectionistic around children who need to make mistakes and learn. Some people are racist, sexist, homophobic, bullying, or just plain mean. There are people who just have no idea how to handle being with children. Some people have drastic personality changes after accidents, illnesses, or head injuries. Some people are reacting to difficult childhoods or have had severe trauma. In the end, the reason why doesn't matter. You and/or your students need to be protected, no matter what.

There are people who join careers, jobs, occupations, clubs, groups, and other organizations that deal with children specifically to prey on them. There aren't that many of them, but they do exist. And they may be the most trusted individuals in society such as police officers, scouting leaders, clergy members, coaches, maybe even members of your own family. These people are very good at pretending. They act one way in public, and in a very different way in private. These people cut across all religions, skin colors, creeds, genders, political spectrums, socioeconomic classes, and professions. Some of the people that we have trusted the most have gone to prison for what they have done to abuse others.

Abuse doesn't have to be physical or sexual. They can be purveyors of hate speech, people who have no interest in facts and throw out inflammatory opinions as fact. Manipulators, liars, cheats, and thieves are out there. "Bombers" try to find meetings, educational events, and other online gatherings and invade the call with whatever would be the most disturbing, such as images of sex, drugs, or drinking.

There are plenty of scammers out there who want to take your money. Some are programs that are not accredited, and/or promise brilliant kids but are really just pushing some outdated educational theory or software. Some have substandard instruction, add programs that are suddenly shut down, or even have multiple campuses that suddenly shut down because of mismanagement or scams.

You have to do your research. Is the educational institution accredited? Do they actually teach what your student needs to learn in order to graduate from high school? Do they use login codes to prevent call "bombers" from getting in? How is their security software?

This doesn't release you from responsibility as parents. **Use VPNs (virtual private networks), logins, and ad blockers. Use antivirus software on your computers.**

Make sure your kids know not to give out their address or telephone numbers. All virtual rooms should have logins. First names only are allowed in virtual rooms. No other identifying information should be given out, except perhaps a city. If you live in a small town, just say the name of the state or province. **Tell your kids to never, ever give out their passwords or room passcodes.**

Billing Address

Remember that **no one has to have your actual address.** You can use a billing address, which doesn't have to be your home. In many countries, you can buy a small box at the post office, or you can hire someone for a company to handle mail for you. This separates your actual address from your mail. You must ensure that whoever is opening your mail gets it to you either physically or electronically in a timely manner if something shows up you actually need. Most billing is done online now, as well as most documents. So, you shouldn't have to worry about receiving actual mail from most businesses these days.

If you were working with an offline school and you have to be living in that school district to attend, then you do have to give out your student's address. Remember, your billing address does not have to be your house; it could be your office or a post office box. If your child is being tutored, and the child is tutored within the home, then that person should not give out your address. Be sure that someone is there during tutoring. You may also want to speak to your tutor's other students. You can have cameras in your home to watch caregivers and tutors.

The great thing about learning via Skype, Zoom, FaceTime, and KakaoTalk is the cost (free), and everyone is in a safe environment. Furthermore, if you move, your student doesn't have to lose a tutor or teacher. That way, no one has to receive physical addresses.

Teenagers

Teenagers especially may not see a problem with meeting someone in the real world later on, someone knowing a real name or location, and may even want to set up a meeting with someone they've met online. **Older students may not see a problem due to a belief in their own invincibility, their ability to know whom to trust, and**

the perfectly normal rebellion against authority of that particular age. They are also probably craving contact with other people. They may see warnings about predators as being overly paranoid, and that it won't happen to them.

There are various apps and programs that can help you monitor what your students are doing and where they are located. Just remember that teens are very savvy, and may be able to get around these measures with their own countermeasures. The best defense is good communication.

The idea is to be calm, rational, and very clear that predators do exist. There are people that hide behind female usernames who are male, and vice versa. A person can be lying about every single thing about themselves. They may even hire a friend or an actor to pretend to be them on conference calls. This is rare, but it does happen. Teach them about catfishing.

Catfishing

Catfishing is a scam, pretending to be something that you are not online to lure someone into a relationship. This can happen to anyone online. This scam is done for a variety of reasons. The catfisher may get some sort of sick thrill about messing with someone's head, may be a sociopath or pedophile who is targeting certain people, or may be looking to steal money or data. Catfishing destroys a person's trust, and this scam can mess with your head and deplete your bank account.

When your child is old enough to understand, make it clear that **anyone can sit behind a computer screen and type in information that is false.** Some people are liars. I personally don't understand why people would waste their time doing such behavior, but they do. **Make sure your kids know there is a reason why there are rules in place about what they say and do online.** Remember that abusers, catfishers, and scammers are very, very good at getting information from people in a way where it sounds like they're just making conversation. You can be the most intelligent adult in the room and still get scammed by a catfisher.

Remember that catfishers hang out in social media, online boards, and group chats. **Go with your gut. If something looks wrong, it probably is.** If your gut feels wrong, stop whatever it is you are doing, and teach your kids to do the same thing.

Most of all, **protect all of your personal information.** Get very good programs that scan your computer at least every day for viruses and make sure everyone in your household knows what information is okay to give out online and what is not. If anyone asks you or your student for money, the answer is always no. If someone refuses a video chat so you cannot see what they actually look like, they're probably catfishing you. If all the photos posted on an online media account are of someone in group photos shot from very far away, or the shots are blurry, they're probably fake. It's very easy to take a picture off the Internet and put it up on social media.

Trust your intuition. If your gut feels strange, stay away from that person online. Delete that person from all of your accounts. You have to protect yourself and your family.

Naming Accounts

Gmail and other email providers allow you to have as many accounts as you would like. **Create an email address that your student can remember that does not include your kids' last name. The same goes for Skype names.**

VPNs

VPNs, virtual private networks, hide where you are when you are online. Google Chrome has an incognito mode. Some VPNs are free, some are free extensions, and some cost money. Research and investigate them and choose the right one for you. You don't want someone to be able to find you.

Legitimate Contacts

If your students are taking online classes or courses, it should be clearly posted how much they are and if you need any other materials in order to take the class. Research all of that before you take a class. If instructors suddenly say they need more money, that is a serious red flag. That person may also not be the real instructor, but a catfisher sneaking in to get more money from the student. That sort of scam is rare, but it does occur. A person from the class may also attempt to contact you and ask you for money. Don't do it.

Do not let your kids give out any information to other students except the first name that they choose to use. If you want to tell someone your city, and you live in a large metropolitan area, then go ahead and do that. Since many online classes are international, people often just give out the name of whatever country they're in. Some people even take courses while they're traveling.

If the school does contact you asking for more money, be absolutely certain you're speaking to the correct person. This shouldn't happen unless there was some sort of problem with your credit card. Be very careful about that as well. Make sure that you were or weren't charged for your credit card before making another payment.

Credit Card and Banking Fraud

Paying online can be risky because there are people who will steal your credit card number. **Use third-party sites such as PayPal in order to pay money without giving your credit card information directly to an institution.** You can even pay through PayPal without having an account. There are other services like this. **Don't ever give out your bank account information to anyone online. Use online payment services instead that do bank transfers.**

One of the best ways to prevent problems if you do not want to use bank transfers through online payment services is to **get a small secured credit card that is used only for educational expenses and tuition.** This is a great way to track all of your educational expenses, which may be used for tax purposes. The other good thing is that you only put enough on there for your needs, topping it off with a little extra for taxes and surcharges. Then, if thieves get the credit card number, it doesn't help them very much.

You can also get transaction protection software on your computer. You should have your computer swept for viruses daily.

If you are scammed, keep records of everything. Contact your credit card company immediately. Using PayPal, Payoneer, or a similar online payment app and having a separate credit card for educational expenses with a limit just large enough to pay for them may be the best way to handle online transactions of this nature.

Online Communication Rules

Be absolutely certain that you and your kids understand all of the rules. That includes communication asynchronously like emails and chat boards, what papers and projects are supposed to look like, exactly what is involved in each project, and how you and your student are supposed to communicate with the instructor and with other students. Make sure you follow the rules.

Explain to your kids that they should never put anything online they wouldn't want you (the parent) to see. What you post is online forever. It may be possible for friends, family, employers, and other people to find some way of seeing what you posted.

Before you sign on for an educational institution, you should be able to see some examples of reverse teaching (flipped classrooms) or a class, find out what exactly is in the curriculum, discover how your students are to be tested, and understand exactly how your students are supposed to learn. Both you and your students must be comfortable with whatever choices you have made.

Record your calls using the app's software, your cell phone, or another app. This is done so the students can review what was said in order to study or complete projects and to prevent any issues. That doesn't mean you have to review hours of data every night. It does mean you will have proof if an instructor goes rogue. That's very unlikely. Schools jealously guard their reputations. But, there's always one bad instructor to mess it up for everyone else. Because of reverse teaching (flipped classrooms) and call recording, you should have ample proof of what is going on to discuss it with the school or other educational institution.

Conclusion

You can't live with fear being how you run your life. But, you can intelligently make decisions to protect yourself and your kids. There are a wide variety of online predators out there. You can keep yourself, your information, and your students safe by following a few simple rules.

- ❑ Calmly and clearly explain online rules to kids.
- ❑ Watch your teens. Their sense of invulnerability may make them ignore the rules.
- ❑ Don't give out any data that you don't have to give out, like addresses and telephone numbers.
- ❑ Use a post office box as your billing address, if possible.
- ❑ Use first names or even nicknames in classes.
- ❑ Use room codes to get into Zoom calls.
- ❑ Never give out passwords or room codes.
- ❑ Your email address used for school or educational purposes should NOT have your last name or other identifying information in it.
- ❑ If the instructor wants to refer to people in the class by last names, explain why you think this is a bad idea. Explain to the school about identity theft.

❑ Don't believe inflated claims.

❑ Record online lectures and calls using software.

❑ Use a separate card with a low limit in order to pay for educational expenses, or a banking app.

❑ Use online payment services such as PayPal and Payoneer so you can keep your credit card information private.

❑ Never pay money to anyone who asks for it on a chat, message board, etc.

❑ Install software such as VPNs, virus protection, and pop-up blockers on your computers and phones. Some of this software is free, or have low-cost versions.

❑ Never post anything online, even in supposedly "safe" chat rooms or message boards, unless you want the entire world to know.

❑ Anyone online can pretend to be someone else. Make real-time calls and don't believe everything you hear.

❑ Don't be afraid to protect yourself, your data, and your kids.

❑ Listen to your gut. If it seems wrong, it probably is.

Using the Checklist Handouts and Projects Section

Overview

This section is designed to get you started quickly. I listed them in alphabetical order in order for you to find what you may be looking for quickly. Use what you want and leave the rest. When you log into the web page (https://ljhawkeauthor.com/download-list/, password HYKE20), you can then print these out at home or at a copy store. I suggest you print them in black and white unless you want to spend the money on printing in color. I suggest printing them out in black and white for most things, and in color for fun things you reuse. You can always use highlighters or colored pencils to color them yourself! Laminate the colored ones or slip them into clear plastic sheets to write on with erasable whiteboard pens and reuse.

Checklists, Handouts, and Projects Table of Contents

- ❑ Apps and Plugins
- ❑ Blog Writing Worksheet
- ❑ Book Review Worksheet
- ❑ Chore Chart
- ❑ Craft Box Checklist
- ❑ Daily Schedule
- ❑ How to Create a Blocked Schedule
- ❑ How to Make Behavior, Emotion, and Chore Charts
- ❑ Journal Writing Prompt Worksheet
- ❑ Kanban Board Project Checklist
- ❑ Kids' Awesome Reading Checklist
- ❑ KWL Chart Worksheet
- ❑ Online School Choice Worksheet
- ❑ Primary School Book Review Worksheet
- ❑ Play Dough and Glitter Slime Supply Checklist
- ❑ School in a Box Choice Worksheet
- ❑ School Supplies Checklist
- ❑ Self-Care Checklist
- ❑ Story Writing Prompt Worksheet
- ❑ Study and Homework Checklist
- ❑ Weekly and Monthly Chore Chart
- ❑ Writing Prompt Checklist

Apps and Plugins

- ❏ First, **determine if you need Android or Apple apps**. Many creators make both.
- ❏ Then, **find free versions FIRST**. The costs can really add up. If you have the funds, then, by all means, use a more expensive app.
- ❏ **Check reviews and look at screenshots WITH YOUR KIDS**. I personally like "dark" themes. Your kids may like ones with wild colors.
- ❏ **Choose your website portal.** I suggest using Google Chrome because it has so many extensions and because it works seamlessly with Google Docs.
    - ❏ Opera has a built-in VPN (virtual private network).
    - ❏ **Internet Explorer is no longer supported** and has been replaced with Microsoft Edge.
    - ❏ Firefox also works quickly.

Time Management apps

- ❏ **Pomodoro timer apps.** These apps will help you "chunk" the time into segments with alarms that include downtime.

Free networking apps

- ❏ **Skype**
- ❏ **Zoom**–Make sure you watch videos on how to use it, including settings. Learn how to have logins so your students' rooms are very private. There are "bombing trolls" who try to enter calls with no login codes. You can share screens to teach or learn online.
- ❏ **Google Hangouts**

Study Apps

- ❏ **Evernote**–This is a note-taking app. This can be used as a separate app, or as an extension to Google Chrome to clip web pages. This is wonderful when writing papers, saving recipes, and the like.
- ❏ **Google Docs–This is the free clone of Microsoft Office.** Files can be saved into Microsoft Office formats. Be careful when switching from Docs to Office; the files may not look the same. There is Google Docs, where the files are stored. Then there are word processing, spreadsheet, presentation, calendar, and even

form applications you can use within Google Docs. There are also numerous free templates for documents. Join for free and generate a free Gmail account. You can use it on a desktop or cell phone.

- ❏ **Meditation apps**–I use Headspace and pay $10 a month. There are plenty of free apps and even YouTube videos. (Meditate in the morning or evening, or both.)
- ❏ **Quizlet**–You can put in your study questions, answers, and vocabulary. It has flashcards and games to memorize the content. Or, search by the school, name of the class, or textbook to find quizzes other people have made. Your kids can create their own and tell their friends!
- ❏ **White noise generators**–These generate sound without lyrics so you can block out other noise in the house. There are many free ones out there. Mine is called Dark Noise and is $3.99 for Apple.

Chrome Extensions (Plugins)

These bits of code attach to Google Chrome to do various tasks. Many are free. They can do anything from add security, allow you to see PDFs, take notes, screen and video capture, and more. Be very careful when deciding to use paid extensions. They may be worth it, but the costs do add up. Other operating systems have their plugins; do your research.

- ❏ **Nimbus**–The free version lets you take desktop screenshots. This extension allows students to take a virtual picture of a lesson or website and put it into another document. I take screenshots of instructors' slides for my notes. The paid version, which at the time of this writing is $14.99 a year, allows users to make screenshot videos of what is on the screen and your voiceover. There is other free screen capture software as well.
- ❏ **VPNs**–Virtual private networks offer security because they hide where you are. Parents use them to make sure trolls can't find where their students live. Expats use them to see and access programs they can't find in the countries where they are located. Some VPNs are free.
- ❏ **Ad/pop-up blockers**–These prevent unwanted pop-ups and redirects to ads. This is a must-have. I use three free ones. I can always "whitelist" a website to enable pop-ups.
- ❏ **Grammarly**–Grammarly has a beta version at the time of this writing that will check spelling and grammar in Google Docs. Google Docs checks this as well, but having a "second opinion" can help.

- **Password Extensions**–Password extensions like LastPass can help you make different passwords for all your websites and keep them in a vault. Student information should remain private!
- **Website Blockers**–Strictly Pomodoro will only let students be on websites for 25 minutes, with a 5-minute break. Parents or students can also block certain websites during study time. StayFocused puts limits on distracting social media websites. These extensions keep people from falling into an Internet "black hole."
- **Quiz programs**–Quizlet lets students put together a study pack on its website. Memorize! is an extension that allows students to put in a list of questions and answers that pop up at various intervals.
- **Google Docs PDF/PowerPoint Viewer**–This extension lets you look at PDFs and slides without having to open another program.

BLOG WRITING WORKSHEET

Name:

Date:

Section:

Subject:

For this blog, I will discuss:

A BOOK REVIEW

BOOK TITLE

NAME

GRADE

SUMMARY

WHO ARE THE CHARACTERS IN THE STORY?

WHAT IS YOUR FAVORITE PART OF THE BOOK?

DID YOU LIKE THE BOOK? WHY OR WHY NOT?

I RATE THIS BOOK _ OUT OF 5

☆ ☆ ☆ ☆ ☆

CHORE CHART

WEEKLY
CHECKLIST

CHORE	PERSON	M	T	W	TH	F

CRAFT BOX CHECKLIST

- Paper
- Construction Paper
- Crepe/Tissue Paper
- Copy Paper
- Stick Glue
- Glitter Glue
- Kids' Scissors
- Crayons
- Washable markers
- Pencils
- Colored pencils
- Erasers
- Watercolor paint
- Paintbrushes
- Paint sponges
- Felt
- Pom poms
- Googly eyes
- Craft string
- Cup for brushes
- Popsicle sticks
- Pipe cleaners
- Modeling clay
- Whiteboard and whiteboard pens

DAILY SCHEDULE   DATE   /   /

MORNING	AFTERNOON	NIGHT

TO DO	NOTES
○	
○	
○	
○	
○	
○	
○	
○	
○	

How to Create a Time Blocked Schedule Worksheet

- ❏ List your daily priorities.
- ❏ Make a list of time-intensive and short tasks.
- ❏ Include breaks and meals.
- ❏ Group these tasks together, like kids, chores, meals, work, etc. **These are your blocks**.
- ❏ Weave short tasks in between the longer ones, or block lots of little tasks together.
- ❏ Decide where in the day these blocks should go, such as morning, afternoon, or evening. You can also have blocks for when the kids go to bed.
- ❏ You may need different blocks for days off, or eliminate most blocks altogether.
- ❏ If there are multiple parents, coordinate schedules or trade off blocks.

Sample Morning:

Meditation/prayer/centering
Spiritual readings
Make the bed
Exercise
Oversee kids' first chore, like sorting laundry
Breakfast
Get older kids started
Sit down with younger kids
Short-chore time
Snack time
Kids' play while you prep lunch

Once you have your tasks and blocks in place, you can then map out your blocked day.

You can print another one for kids if you like.

You can shade in or draw a box around each block. This gives you a clear picture of what tasks are supposed to be done at what time of day.

Laminate the page or slide it into a plastic sheet cover. Either fill it out first or leave it blank if you want to write on it with an erasable whiteboard marker rather than filling out the tasks directly on the page. You may need to change it several times until it is exactly the way you want.

Remember that some tasks are biweekly or monthly. I suggest having a master calendar, electronic or paper, that has these "pop-up events" in them.

Block Schedule

Time	Monday	Tuesday	Wednesday	Thursday	Friday	Saturday	Sunday
5:00							
6:00							
7:00							
8:00							
9:00							
10:00							
11:00							
12:00							
1:00							
2:00							
3:00							
4:00							
5:00							
6:00							
7:00							
8:00							
9:00							
10:00							
11:00							
12:00							

How to Make Behavior, Emotion, and Chore Charts

Behavior Chart

Behavior charts are useful for younger kids or kids with autism or other behavioral issues. I would go simple here.

- ❑ Take a piece of printer paper.
- ❑ Use red, green, and yellow, the same as a stoplight.
- ❑ Write "What is my behavior today?" on the side of the sheet in block letters.
- ❑ Then, draw three huge circles vertically on the right side.
- ❑ Color the bottom one green, the middle one yellow, and the top one red. Be sure the colors are not too dark so you can see the faces.
- ❑ Draw a happy face on the bottom, a so-so face in the middle, and a sad face in the top circle.
- ❑ Slide the paper into a plastic protector or laminate it.
- ❑ Use washi tape to attach it to the wall, or attach velcro or a suction cup to a door.
- ❑ Use a clothespin to show the child's behavior.

Emotion Chart

These charts are all over the Internet. You can print one out. Or use icons to create one and either draw the icons on blank printer paper or poster board, or print it out on your computer.

How to create your own emotion chart:

- ❑ Go to www.iconfinder.com. Type in "emotions" then select "free" on the left-hand side.
- ❑ If you want to print out your poster, download the free icon and upload it to your document or presentation slide.
- ❑ If you want to draw it, make a grid on your paper. I would select a 3x4 or 4x4 grid. If you want to list more emotions, make more boxes in your grid! To make creating grids easier, use a ruler, or you can use dot or graph paper underneath.
- ❑ Draw one icon in each box.
- ❑ Label each box.
- ❑ Slide it into a sheet protector.
- ❑ Use washi tape to attach it to the wall, or attach velcro or a suction cup to a door.
- ❑ Use reusable stickers or erasable whiteboard pens to mark emotions.

Chore Chart

First, research images online. There are printable chore charts, or you can order a board sent to you online with icons of the chores on them.

Create Your Own Chore Chart:

Simple chart:
- Use notebook or blank paper.
- Write Chores on the top.
- Underneath, write Chores on the left-hand side.
- Halfway across, write M T W TH F S Su.
- Draw grid lines straight down on the days of the week.
- Draw grid lines across for the chores.
- Since chores are rotated or change as the child gets older, leave the chores blank for now.
- If you want to get colorful, color in the days of the week.
- Slide the chart into a plastic sheet protector or laminate it.
- Fill in the chores and who does them on each line with erasable whiteboard pens.
- Use washi tape to attach it to the wall, or attach velcro or a suction cup to a door.
- Use stickers or erasable whiteboard pens when a chore is done.

Complex Chart:
- Go to www.iconfinder.com. Type in "chores" then select "free" on the left-hand side.
- If you want to print out your poster, download the free icon and upload it to your document or presentation slide.
- If you want to draw it, use blank paper.
- Turn the paper to the side to write in landscape, not portrait mode.
- Write I Did It or Done on the top and the person's name.
- The left-hand side is for icons of the chores, and their names, such as Make Bed or Sweep Room.
- You will need a grid of 9 boxes across (the first two boxes make one unit per line) and as many as you want down (maybe seven or eight).
- Spell out the days of the week in the last seven boxes on top.
- Draw grid lines straight down on the days of the week.
- Draw grid lines across for the chores.

- ❏ If you want to get colorful, color the days of the week and/or the icons of the chores.
- ❏ Slide the chart into a plastic sheet protector or laminate it.
- ❏ Make one chart for each member of the family.
- ❏ Use washi tape to attach each one to the wall, or attach velcro or a suction cup to a door.
- ❏ Hang up your charts.
- ❏ Use stickers or erasable whiteboard pens when a chore is done.

Tip: If you prefer to use magnets, run strips of magnetic tape behind the columns of days of the week.

Tip: Have the stickers, checks, circles, or magnets mean something! Kids can trade them in for special time with parents, non-educational movies or games, being able to pick a game first on game night, etc.

Tip: Parents need their own chore charts so kids learn everyone has chores! It also helps with chore rotation if you choose that system. Keep them simple so you don't get bogged down.

NAME

SECTION

DATE

TEACHER

JOURNAL WRITING PROMPT

Write what happened today using the prompts below.

What was the best part of your day?
What was the worst part of your day?
What happened today that you would like to change?

Kanban Board
Project Checklist

- [ ] Cardboard (mine is 48 x 54cm (19 x 21in)
- [ ] Whiteboard or other contact paper
- [ ] Washi tape
- [ ] Sticky notes or strips
- [ ] Back of door or wall hook
- [ ] Cord OR lanyard
- [ ] Attach lanyard/cord w/glue or tape
- [ ] Cover cardboard w/contact paper
- [ ] Washi tape the outside
- [ ] Divide into segments w/washi tape
- [ ] Divide large tasks into small ones
- [ ] Write tasks on sticky notes
- [ ] Put sticky notes onto board
- [ ] Done tasks in can/cup lead to reward

Kids' Awesome Reading List

- ☐ **CLASSICS**

- ☐ **FICTION**

- ☐ **NONFICTION**

- ☐ **POETRY**

- ☐ **ACTION/ADVENTURE**

- ☐ **HISTORY**

I know that...

I want to know about...

I learned that...

Online School Choice Worksheet

First, look on the schools' websites. Start a notebook sheet or a spreadsheet using this template.

If you don't like a column, change it! This is a guide. Alter it to fit the needs of your kids.

Name of School	Cost per (year, semester)	Live vs. reverse/ flipped teaching (time zones?)	How to turn in work	Gifted and/or Advanced Placement classes (Y/N)	International Baccalaureate program (Y/N)	Specials: Art/ Music/ Languages/ Drama/ Coding

More questions:
- ❏ **Be sure they are fully accredited before doing any further research.**
- ❏ **Be sure that the school placement test and all of the academics are online.**
- ❏ **Find out if the school offers assistance or tutoring for struggling students and help for students with learning differences**. Is this free or an extra cost? You may have to hire a tutor to help your students.
- ❏ **Find out if you can join anytime, or if you must wait until the next semester.**

Top Three: ___________________________________

  ____

  ____

Best Choice: ___________________________________

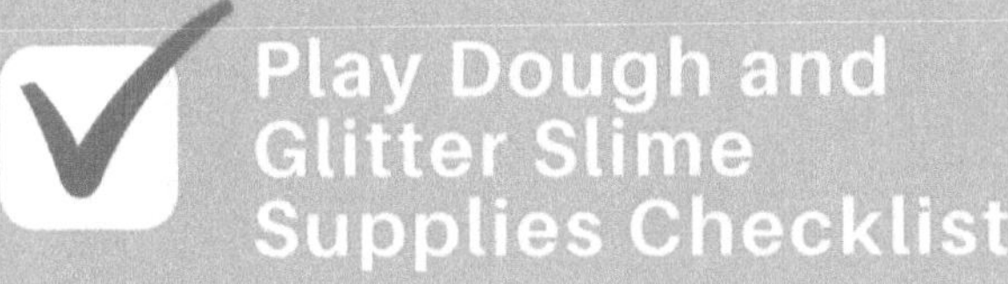

- [ ] Flour
- [ ] Cream of tartar
- [ ] Salt
- [ ] Vegetable oil
- [ ] Gel food coloring
- [ ] Water
- [ ] Saucepan and stove
- [ ] Glitter school glue
- [ ] Baking soda
- [ ] Contact lens solution
- [ ] Storage containers/zip bags
- [ ] https://glitterinc.com/how-to-make-3-ingredient-glitter-slime/
- [ ] domesticsuperhero.com/best-homemade-playdough-recipe/

A BOOK REVIEW

Book Title and Author

SUMMARY
OF THE BOOK

WHAT DO YOU LIKE MOST
ABOUT THE STORY?

WILL YOU RECOMMEND THIS
BOOK TO YOUR FRIENDS?

WHAT DO YOU LIKE LEAST
ABOUT THE STORY?

School in a Box School Choice Worksheet

First, look on the curriculum vendors' websites. Start a notebook sheet or a spreadsheet using this template.

If you don't like a column, change it! This is a guide. Alter it to fit the needs of your students.

Name of Provider	Cost per (year, entire K-12)	Other resources (videos, online lessons)	Gifted and/or IB/ Advanced Placement content (Y/N)	Special considerations (environmental, religion, language)	Specials: Art/ Music/ Languages/ Drama/ Coding

More questions:
- ❏ **Be sure they fully cover what your district/country requires for that grade.**
- ❏ **Do they require a school placement test?**

Top Three: ____________________________

____

____

Best Choice: ____________________________

☐ Paper	**NOTES**
☐ Pencils	
☐ Pencil lead	
☐ Erasers	
☐ Ballpoint pens	
☐ Pencil Box	
☐ Colored Pencils	
☐ Stick Glue	
☐ Kids' Scissors	
☐ Crayons	
☐ Washable markers	
☐ Wide-ruled notebooks/pads	
☐ Plastic folders	
☐ Construction paper	
☐ Ruler	
☐ Correction tape	
☐ Highlighters	
☐ Three-ring binder	
☐ Spiral notebooks OR paper	
☐ Graph paper	
☐ Graphing calculator	
☐ Post-its	
☐ Index cards	
☐ Subject dividers	

self-care check-in

**CHECK THE BOXES OF THE ACTIVITIES
DAILY TO TAKE CARE OF YOURSELF.**

- [ ] EAT THREE MAIN MEALS
- [ ] WRITE IN A JOURNAL
- [ ] READ A BOOK
- [ ] FIND A QUIET SPOT TO MEDITATE
- [ ] LIGHT AN AROMATIC CANDLE
- [ ] DO A GRATITUDE LIST
- [ ] PRACTICE DEEP BREATHING
- [ ] LISTEN TO GOOD MUSIC
- [ ] EXERCISE
- [ ] CATCH UP WITH A FRIEND
- [ ] CALL A FAMILY MEMBER
- [ ] SPEND TIME OUTDOORS
- [ ] HAVE A MINI PAMPER SESSION
- [ ] CUDDLE A CHILD AND/OR PET
- [ ] TRY SOMETHING NEW
- [ ] TAKE A COURSE OR CLASS

Make it a habit to take care of yourself

NAME: _______________________________________

SECTION: _____________ DATE: _____________ SCORE: _____________

Story Writing

Let your imagination run wild with a story!

Story Idea:

Checklist

STUDY & HOMEWORK

- Math
- Science
- History
- Social Studies
- Art
- Music
- Foreign Language

MY WEEKLY CHORES

HOUSE CHORES

M	T	W	TH	F

CHORES IN MY ROOM

M	T	W	TH	F

OTHER STUFF

M	T	W	TH	F

Name: _______________________   Year and Section: _______________________

Submitted to: _______________________   Date: _______________________

Write an essay using the following sentence starters:

Thank you!

Thank you for being one of my beautiful, amazing readers! I can't do what I do without you! If you liked the book, please leave a review! I read them all, looking to improve my craft so I can write more helpful books for you.

Thank you to my beta reader, Christine Bumgardner, a teacher and professor extraordinaire, and an excellent friend. My editor, talented_fixer, is amazing. Any errors left in the manuscript are entirely my own. Please let me know what they are in your online review so I can fix them! Or, you can contact me on social media at Facebook: Facebook.com/lj.hawke, Instagram: Instagram.com/ljhawke, and Twitter: Twitter.com/Hawkelj, and my website: ljhawkeauthor.com.

Books in the Hack Your Education series:

Hack Your Kids' Education
Hack Your Own Education

About the Author

L. J. Hawke is an author and university professor. She has over a decade of experience teaching PreK-12, in person and online. She has a master's degree in business administration and a dual master's degree in education and bilingual education, with an emphasis in online education. She writes nonfiction titles in her fields of expertise, as well as various fiction novels. She can be found teaching her students, petting her cats while writing, or with a backpack on her back, traveling the world—after calling the cat sitter.

One last thing…

If you enjoyed this book or found it useful, I'd be very grateful if you'd post a short review on Amazon. Your support really does make a difference, and I read all the reviews personally so I can get your feedback and make this book even better.

Thanks again for your support!